Building A Dynamic Team

A Practical Guide To
Maximizing Team Performance

Richard Y. Chang

First published in 1994 by Richard Chang Associates, Inc., USA.

This edition published in 1995 by Kogan Page Ltd.

Kogan Page Limited
120 Pentonville Road
London N1 9JN

British Library Cataloguing in Publication Data

A CIP record for this book is available from the British Library.

ISBN 0 7494 1663 7

Printed and bound in Great Britain by
Biddles Ltd, Guildford and King's Lynn

1

Acknowledgments

About The Author

Richard Y. Chang is President and CEO of Richard Chang Associates, Inc., a diversified organizational improvement consulting firm based in Irvine, California. He is internationally recognized for his management strategy, quality improvement, organization development, customer satisfaction, and human resource development expertise.

The author would like to acknowledge the support of the entire team of professionals at Richard Chang Associates, Inc. for their contribution to the guidebook development process. In addition, special thanks are extended to the many client organizations who have helped us shape the practical ideas and proven methods shared in this guidebook.

Additional Credits

Editor: Scott Rimmer

Reviewer: Sarah Ortlieb Fraser and Ruth Stingley

Graphic Layout: Suzanne Jamieson

Cover Design: John Odam Design Associates

PREFACE

The 1990's have already presented individuals and organizations with some very difficult challenges to face and overcome. So who will have the advantage as we move toward the year 2000 and beyond?

The advantage will belong to those with a commitment to continuous learning. Whether on an individual basis or as an entire organization, one key ingredient to building a continuous learning environment is *The Practical Guidebook Collection* brought to you by the Publications Division of Richard Chang Associates, Inc.

After understanding the future *"learning needs"* expressed by our clients and other potential customers, we are pleased to publish *The Practical Guidebook Collection*. These guidebooks are designed to provide you with proven, *"real-world"* tips, tools, and techniques—on a wide range of subjects—that you can apply in the workplace and/or on a personal level immediately.

Once you've had a chance to benefit from *The Practical Guidebook Collection*, please share your feedback with us. We've included a brief *Evaluation and Feedback Form* at the end of the guidebook that you can fax to us.

With your feedback, we can continuously improve the resources we are providing through the Publications Division of Richard Chang Associates, Inc.

Wishing you successful reading,

Richard Y. Chang
President and CEO
Richard Chang Associates, Inc.

TABLE OF CONTENTS

CHAPTER ONE

INTRODUCTION

Have you ever watched a real team in action? No, not the team with the hotshot player who corners the ball and makes every basket. That team may win today's game, but at what expense? No, a real team features players who play well together, are positioned correctly, and who consistently win as the result of team effort. Real teams usually make it to the play-offs.

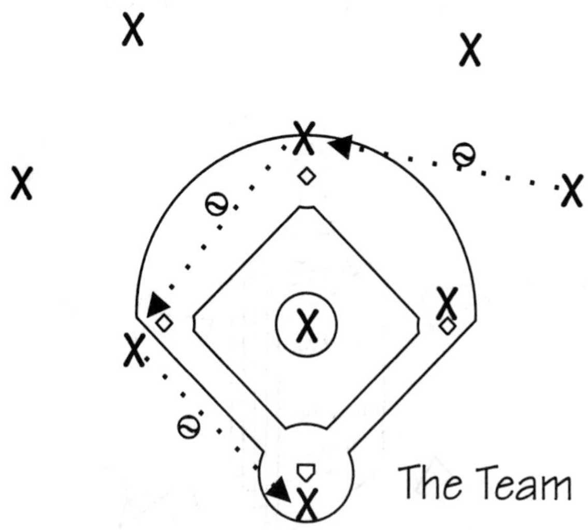

What's true about real teams in sports is also true in business. Often a group presented as a team is nothing more than a collection of individuals who don't know the first thing about how to function together. That group hasn't been given the opportunity to become a team. With no practice sessions scheduled and having been relegated to the sidelines, they're shooting in the dark.

It takes effort, conscious effort, to mold a group of individuals into a dynamic, high-performance team. But the rewards are worth every moment of planning, practice, and persistence!

Why Read This Guidebook?

Maybe you've just formed a new team and you want it to excel. Perhaps you want to revitalize your department. Or maybe your group is in the midst of a long-term project and at its current rate, it won't reach your goals on time. In business, any kind of delay costs money, as well as time.

Whether you desire to build a new team or reconstruct one already in operation, owning a *"playbook"* is essential to your success. Use this guidebook as your playbook. It will help you change your group from a collection of individuals into a collaborative team.

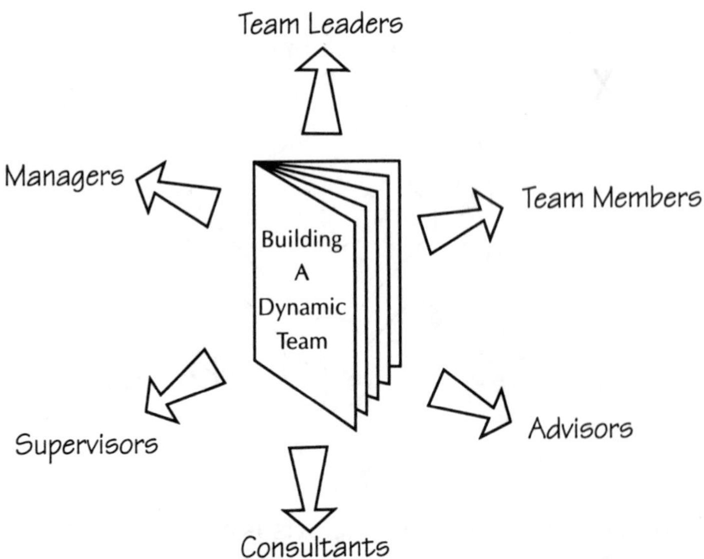

Who Should Read This Guidebook?

Anyone involved with teams will benefit from reading this guidebook. Team leaders, members, and advisors can use this book to boost their teams' productivity. Managers and supervisors can teach their departments how to work together as a committed team. Consultants can lead teams to success. If you're ready to create a new, dynamic team or rejuvenate an unproductive one, you're ready for this guidebook.

When And How To Use It

Use this guidebook at any stage of team development. A newly formed team will get off to a good start by following these guidelines, and it will be headed in the right direction. An ineffective team can veer back on course, stimulated by a whole new focus. You can even use this guidebook to evaluate a team in progress and identify ways to improve it. Or you can use it to minimize disruption when team members leave, new ones are hired, or whenever change affects your team.

The guidelines in this guidebook aren't a set of rigid, exact rules. No two teams are alike, so you need to be flexible in working with your particular team. *Building A Dynamic Team* allows for this flexibility; the examples, points, worksheets, and forms are designed to be adaptable to your own unique situation.

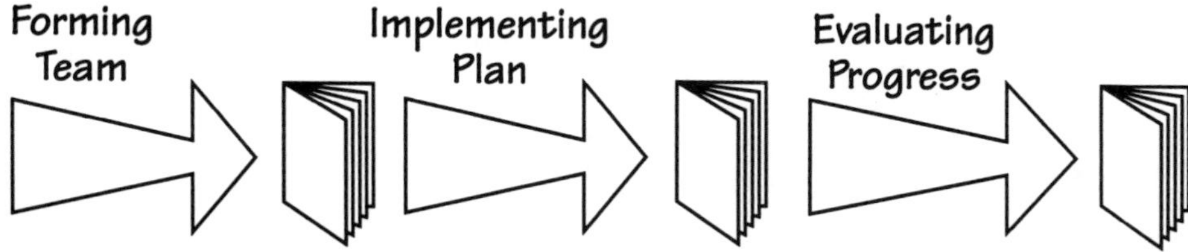

Note: You may be interested in additional guidebooks that supplement the information provided in this one. Consider reading the following guidebooks to increase your expertise in creating dynamic teams:

Success Through Teamwork

Team Decision-Making Techniques

Measuring Team Performance

Meetings That Work!

Coaching Through Effective Feedback

THE ELEMENTS OF A DYNAMIC TEAM

A dynamic team is a high-performance team, one that utilizes its energy to produce. It's a confident team, one whose members are aware of their strengths and use them to reach their goals. And it's a team whose members rely on each other for assistance, feedback, and motivation. A dynamic team stands out from other teams.

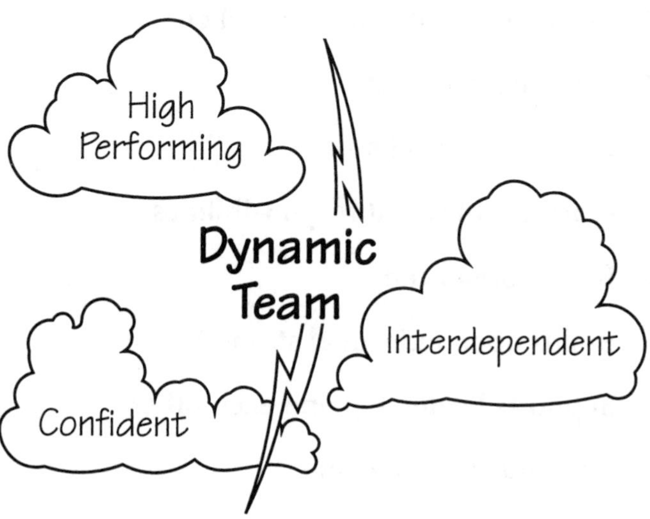

All dynamic teams have certain key characteristics in common. Read through the following list to understand what makes dynamic teams distinctive. You'll know what to strive for if you're in the process of forming a team, or you can use the list to assess an existing team's strengths and weaknesses.

A Dynamic Team . . .

- Clearly states its mission and goals
- Operates creatively
- Focuses on results
- Clarifies roles and responsibilities
- Is well-organized
- Builds upon individual strengths
- Supports leadership and each other
- Develops team climate
- Resolves disagreements
- Communicates openly
- Makes objective decisions
- Evaluates its own effectiveness

The Critical Elements

Now we'll explore each element of a dynamic team. A dynamic team is one that:

Clearly states its mission and goals

A team requires a clearly stated purpose and goals; not just an understanding of what needs to be done at the moment, but an understanding of the overall focus of the team. Shared goals and objectives lead to commitment. Leaders of a dynamic team make sure that all members are involved in defining their team's goals.

Operates creatively

Experimentation and creativity are vital signs of a dynamic team. Such teams take calculated risks by trying different ways of doing things. They aren't afraid of failure, and they look for opportunities to implement new processes or techniques. They're also flexible and creative when dealing with problems and making decisions.

Focuses on results

The ability to produce what is required, when it is required, is the true test. A dynamic team is capable of achieving results beyond the sum of its individual members. Team members continually meet time, budget, and quality commitments. *"Optimum productivity"* is a shared goal.

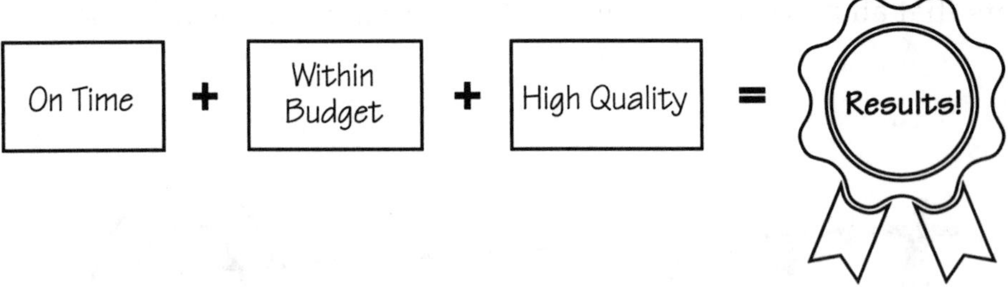

Clarifies roles and responsibilities

A dynamic team clarifies roles and responsibilities for all its members. Each team member knows what is expected of him or her, and knows the roles of fellow team members. A dynamic team updates its roles and responsibilities to keep up with changing demands, objectives, and technology.

Roles & Responsibilities Team Member A

- ☑ ____________
- ☑ ____________
- ☑ ____________
- ☑ ____________

Is well-organized

A dynamic team defines protocol, procedures, and policies from the very beginning. Structure allows a team to meet the demands of any tasks it must handle.

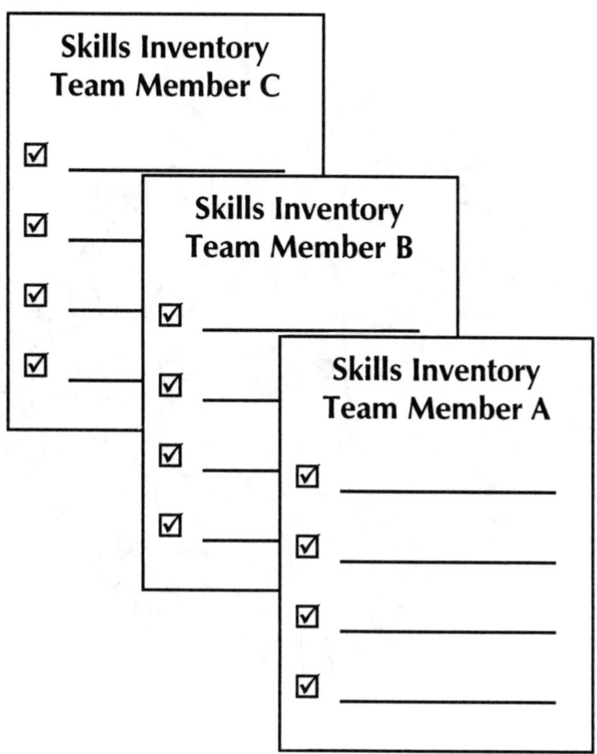

Builds upon individual strengths

Coaches of sports teams constantly inventory their players' skills. Likewise, leaders of dynamic business teams regularly catalog their team's knowledge, skills, and talents. Team leaders are aware of their members' strengths and weaknesses, so they can effectively draw upon individual competencies.

Supports leadership and each other

Dynamic teams share leadership roles among members. Such teams give every member the opportunity to *"shine"* as the leader. The team members also appreciate formal supervisory roles, because the formal leaders of a dynamic team support team efforts and respect individual uniquenesses.

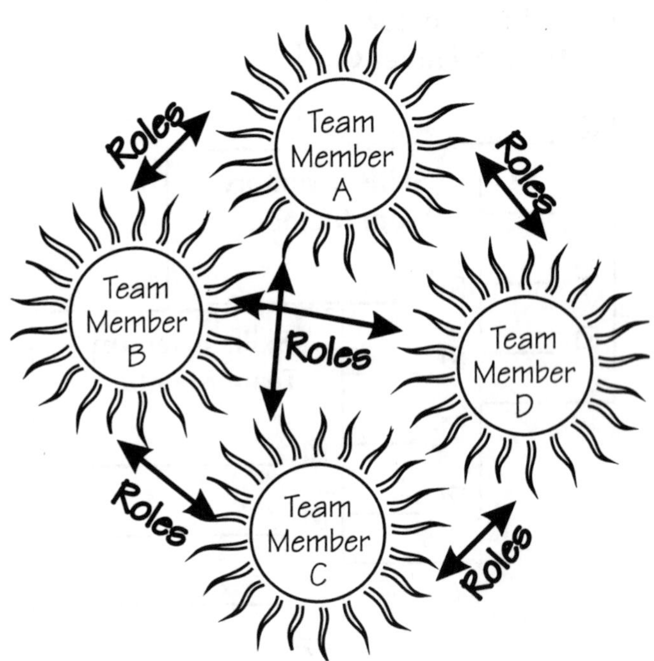

Develops team climate

A high-performance team has members who enthusiastically work well together with high degrees of involvement and group energy (*i.e., synergy*). Collectively, individual members feel more productive and find that team activities renew their interest and spirit. Such a team develops a distinct character of its own.

Resolves disagreements

Disagreement occurs in all teams. It's not necessarily bad or destructive. A dynamic team deals openly with conflict when it occurs. The team members recognize conflict and try to resolve it through honest discussions tempered by mutual trust.

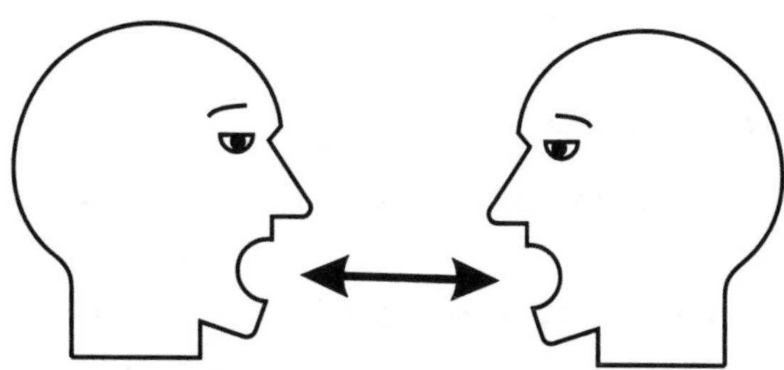

Communicates openly

Members of a dynamic team talk to each other directly and honestly. Each person solicits suggestions from other members, fully considers what they say, and then builds on their ideas.

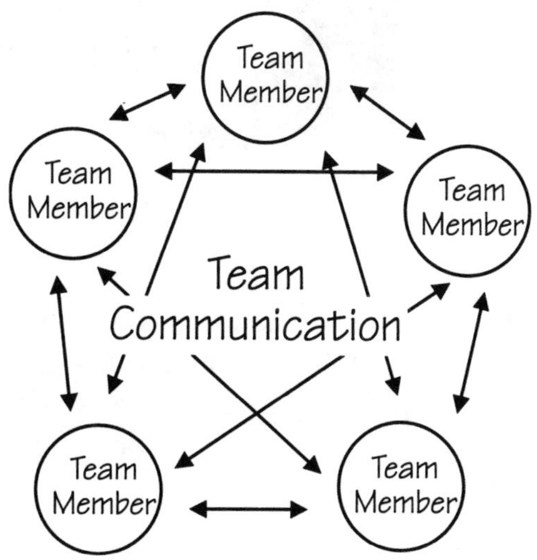

Makes objective decisions

Dynamic teams have well-established, proactive approaches to solving problems and making decisions. Decisions are reached through consensus; everybody must be able to *"live with"* and willingly support the decisions. Members feel free to express their feelings about any decision. The team members clearly understand and accept all decisions, and they come up with contingency (*back-up*) plans.

Evaluates its own effectiveness

A team needs to routinely examine itself to see how it's doing. *"Continuous improvement"* and *"proactive management"* are operating philosophies of dynamic teams. If performance problems arise, they can be resolved before they become serious.

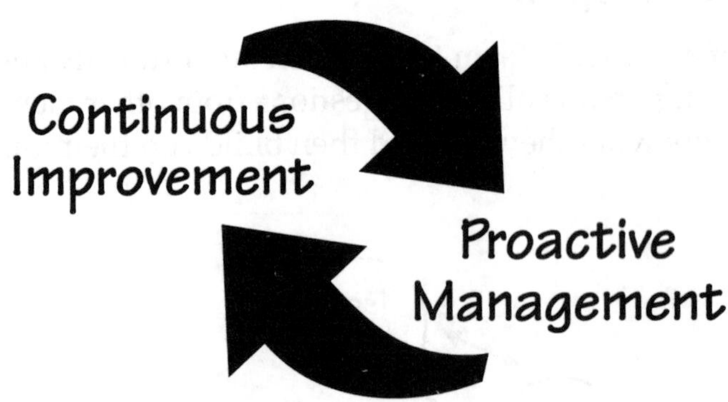

That's quite a list! While it's a rare team that receives top scores on every item, teams that work toward becoming dynamic often achieve high overall marks. If you desire to lead a dynamic team, prepare to embark on a journey that will be rough in spots, but ultimately rewarding.

CHAPTER TWO WORKSHEET: RATING YOUR TEAM

1. Use the following assessment to rate your team (*if you haven't yet formed a team, rate a team you were previously on*). For each characteristic of a dynamic team, rate your team on a scale of 1 to 7; circling a "7" means your team is exceptional, and a "1" means it is deficient.

"Dynamic Team" Assessment

1. Clearly states its mission and goals

   1 2 3 4 5 6 7

2. Operates creatively

   1 2 3 4 5 6 7

3. Focuses on results

   1 2 3 4 5 6 7

4. Clarifies roles and responsibilities

   1 2 3 4 5 6 7

5. Is well-organized

   1 2 3 4 5 6 7

6. Builds upon individual strengths

   1 2 3 4 5 6 7

7. Supports leadership and each other

1 2 3 4 5 6 7

8. Develops team climate

1 2 3 4 5 6 7

9. Resolves disagreements

1 2 3 4 5 6 7

10. Communicates openly

1 2 3 4 5 6 7

11. Makes objective decisions

1 2 3 4 5 6 7

12. Evaluates its own effectiveness

1 2 3 4 5 6 7

Total Score ________________

Interpreting your score:

If your score is 75–84: Congratulations! Your team is at, or near, optimum performance. Maintaining your team at this high level should be your goal.

If your score is 65–74: Not bad! Your team's in pretty good shape, although there is room for improvement.

If your score is 55–64: Your team has problems, some of which may be serious. To rectify them, your team needs to focus on improving its lowest-scoring characteristics.

If your score is 54 or below: Your members are not functioning as a team. Your team needs to work on the basics of team building.

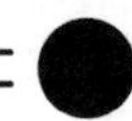

2. Discuss the following with your team:

a) What are your team's strong points? What contributes to these strengths?

b) What are your team's areas for improvement? What is contributing to the lack of high scores in these areas?

3. What ideas do you have for becoming a more dynamic team?

BUILDING A DYNAMIC TEAM

Are you and your team members ready to build a dynamic team? If so, you'll need a model to guide your team to its final destination. Your specific route may vary somewhat, depending on your team, but all teams that become dynamic cover roughly the same terrain.

Primary Phases Of Team Development

Building a dynamic team includes the following four primary phases of development:

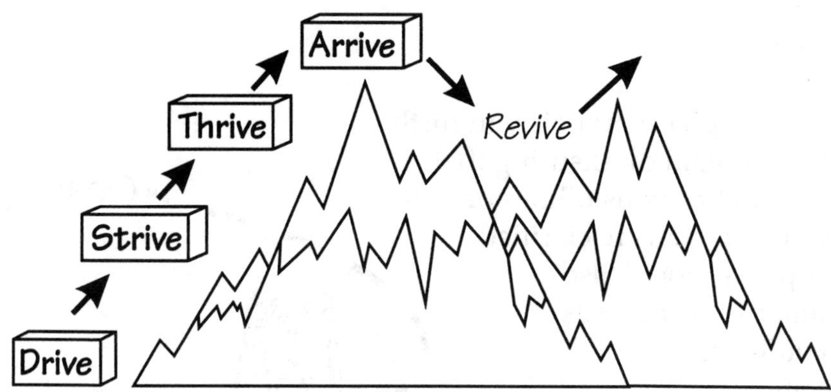

You can visualize the process as stages in mountain climbing. A dynamic team requires planning, strategy, and downright hard work to conquer a mountain. You won't be able to scale the peak overnight, but if your team works diligently, every upward move, however slow, will be exhilarating.

Clearly, once you've reached the peak of team performance, or if you slip backward along the way, it's important to continue *"reviving"* the team to maintain peak performance.

Drive

In the driving phase, your team will focus on its mission and establish guidelines for the *"journey."* You'll be taking the critical first step up the mountain by choosing your goals, priorities, and *"rules of the road."*

Strive

The striving phase propels you further up the mountain by ensuring that the roles and responsibilities of all team members are clarified. In this phase, you'll also encounter some hazards that you'll need to overcome.

Thrive

The thriving phase causes productivity to rapidly increase. Your team transcends difficulties by utilizing peer feedback, conflict management, collaboration, and effective decision making. You're covering territory fast and effectively, making it up the mountain by sheer force and persistence.

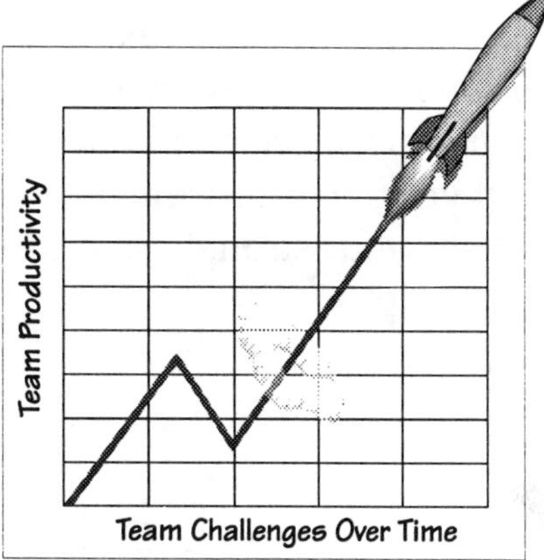

Arrive

In the last phase—arriving—your team reaches the mountaintop. You've reached a level of peak performance. You truly function as a dynamic team.

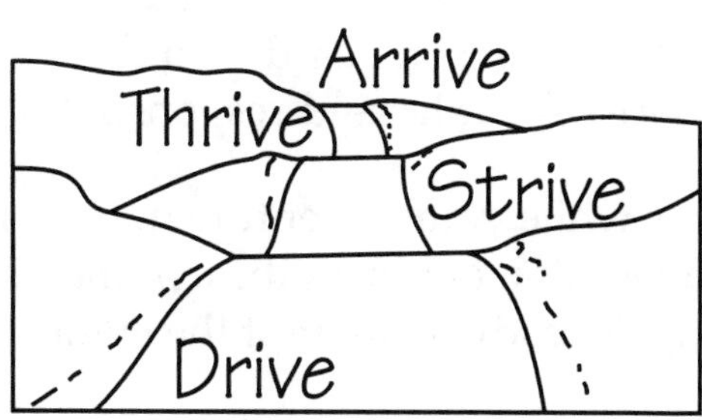

And then, revive

Now here's the clincher: rarely does a team make it up the mountain on the first try. Each step in the process leads you closer to becoming a dynamic team. But in the real world, unwelcome intrusions or changes often disrupt even the most thorough plans. What happens if two of your team members quit the team? Or what if your organization decides to restructure your department? Suddenly, your stronghold on the mountain weakens and you begin to slip.

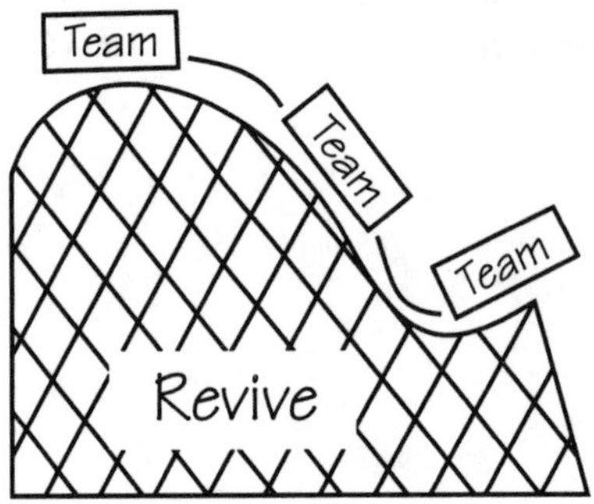

When this happens, your team should go into a reviving mode, where you backtrack some steps to regroup. For example, if there is a restructuring in your department, you'll have to reestablish your team's goals and priorities. So, you'll return to phase one, where you'll focus your team on a mission. If you lose members and others come on board, you'll have to return to phase two and clarify the roles and responsibilities again.

So, while your adventure may be rife with obstacles, it will also abound in opportunities. In the next chapter, we'll look at one team that's ready to attempt the climb.

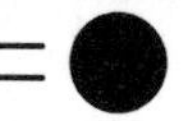

CHAPTER THREE WORKSHEET: YOUR TEAM'S CLIMB TO THE TOP

1. Based on the results of the *"Dynamic Team"* Assessment in the last chapter, which of the four primary phases of development is your team currently in?

2. What challenges do you foresee in moving through the four primary phases?

3. Which phase will offer the greatest opportunity for increasing team performance?

Microsales, Inc.: Tackling The Team Concept

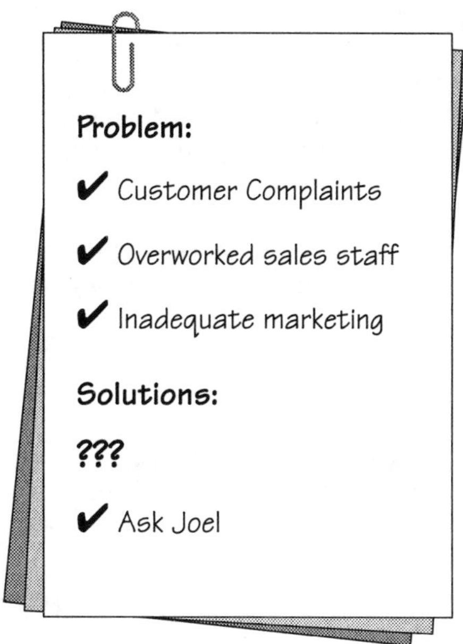

Microsales, Inc. was in the process . . .

of expanding their product line to offer a greater variety of computer components. Customers began flooding Microsales' phone lines with queries regarding the new components. However, their small Sales and Marketing department, which was already inundated with work, couldn't adequately respond to the customers. The sales/marketing personnel were often at a loss in answering the questions, and they were unable to recommend a number of the new products.

The president of the organization called Joel, the department manager, into her office. *"Joel,"* she began, *"we're backed up against the wall with customer complaints."* She motioned for Joel to sit down, then she shook her head. *"I know, I know, you don't have to say it. We haven't done a great job of handling the changes. But we need your department to rectify the situation."*

When Joel left the office, he muttered to himself, *"That's easy for her to say. But I'm the one who's ultimately responsible. Now I have to manage a miracle in the most overworked department in the organization."*. . .

Joel, along with the other managers . . .
in his organization, had recently attended a seminar on team development. *"Maybe it's time to put theory into practice,"* he mused. *"It'll be a real test to see if my department can actually function as a dynamic team. But I guess it's worth a try."*

Joel asked each representative in his department to attend their first team meeting the following day. Marlee and John, long-time employees of Microsales, Inc., seemed perplexed by Joel's request. Sue scrambled for a notepad and wrote down the time. Armando, juggling a huge manual and a sandwich, blurted out, *"I'll be there."* And Karen, the newest employee, nodded as she fielded yet another call.

Tomorrow, the Microsales Sales and Marketing department would take its first step in becoming a dynamic, high-performing team.

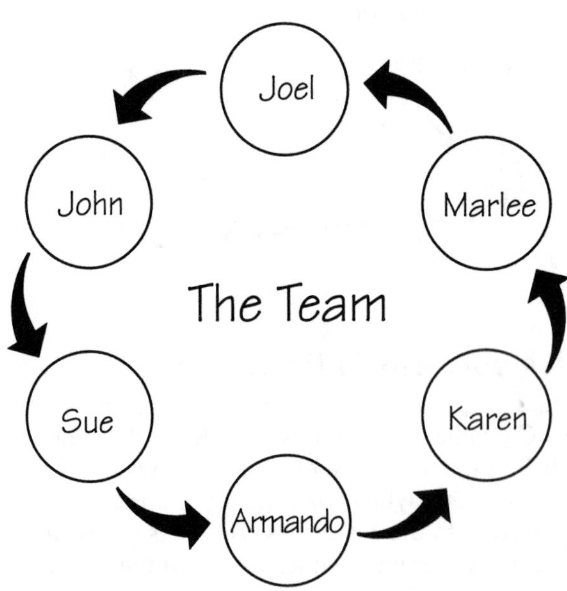

CHAPTER FOUR WORKSHEET: OPPORTUNITIES—YOUR TEAM AND OTHERS

1. What benefits would there be if your team was operating as a dynamic, high-performing team?

2. What problems would be eliminated if your team was operating as a dynamic, high-performing team?

3. Who would be affected by positive changes in your team? How?

Phase One: Driving Toward A Mission

The first phase in building a dynamic team involves focusing individual members on your team's goals. To complete Phase One, driving toward a mission, you need to:

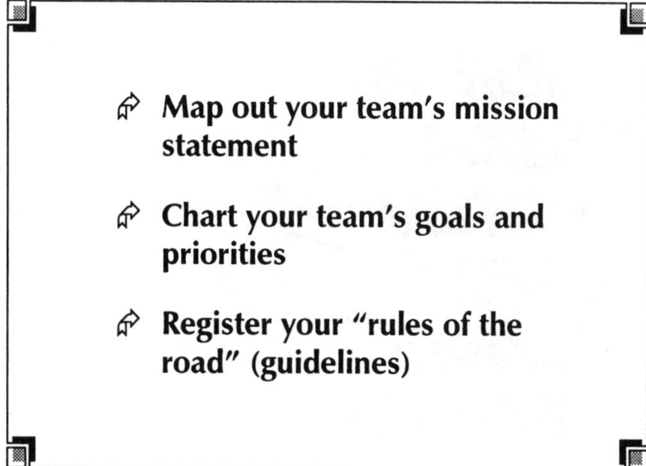

- **Map out your team's mission statement**
- **Chart your team's goals and priorities**
- **Register your "rules of the road" (guidelines)**

Completing these steps will provide you with a solid basis on which you can build team success. If your team is already up and running and you haven't completed these steps, don't delay. This phase lays the groundwork for commitment, an essential characteristic of a dynamic team.

Map Out Your Team's Mission Statement

Agreeing on a team mission statement is comparable to agreeing on a destination. If some members believe conquering Productivity Peak is the key to your team's success, while others think that climbing Mount Mediocre is acceptable, then your team has already cut its performance potential. Your ranks are divided. Your team needs to come to a consensus.

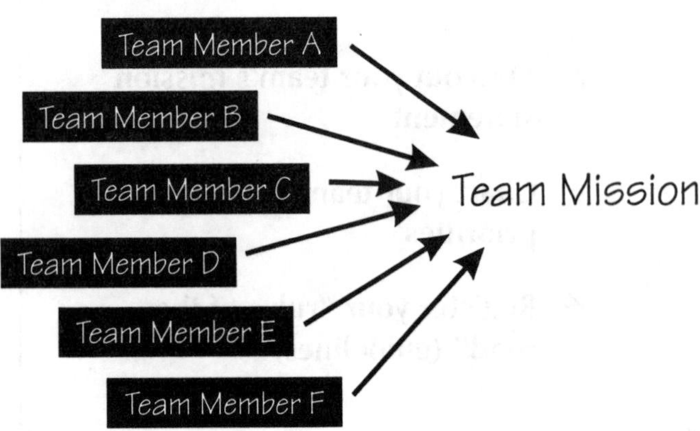

If all of your team members can agree upon the same purpose for your team, their ideas will be focused and their commitment to the team will solidify. Having a team mission unites and motivates employees.

Joel was ready . . .

for his team's first brainstorming session. He knew his group's morale was low, so he had positive statements about each employee already prepared. Joel began the meeting with a flip chart that listed each team member's name: Marlee, John, Sue, Armando, and Karen.

"Okay, team," he said. *"Before we focus on our mission, let's focus on our part in this organization. What things can you think of that we do well?"* Silence prevailed. *"Well, I'll start us off,"* Joel said. *"Marlee and John, both of you have been with Microsales for a long time. I don't think anyone can match your explanations of our computer systems."*

"Until they dumped all the new components on top of us at once," Marlee complained. *"I can't even think straight anymore."*

Joel nodded. *"I realize that the changes have been very difficult for all of us,"* he said. *"But why don't we try to focus on just the positives right now."*

Joel looked over at Sue. *"Sue has a tremendous capacity for handling detail. She'll uncover information on anything you ask her about. And Armando, your patience is exemplary. You're able to deal with the crankiest customers without losing your cool."* Joel paused and motioned at Karen. *"As for Karen, what a fast learner! She's been here only three months, yet she already has a firm understanding of all of our products."*

The session picked up. Joel asked more pertinent questions about their team's mission, and the team members started participating. They came up with several ideas, all of which Joel recorded on the flip chart. . . .

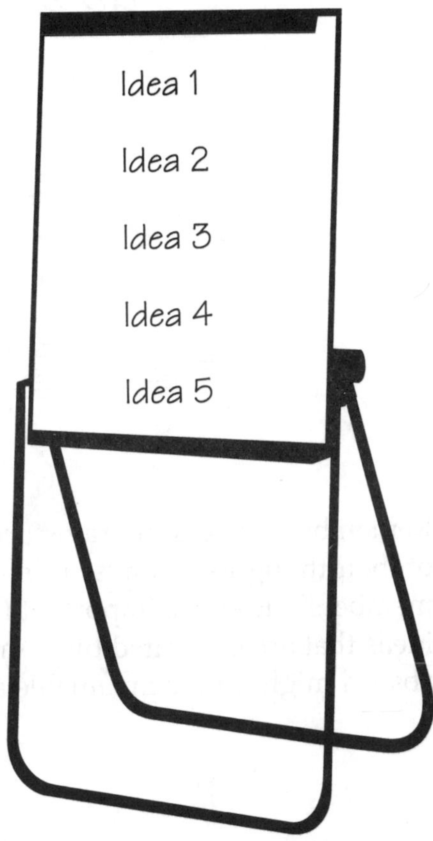

A mission is different from a goal; a mission is a clear statement of *"why your team exists,"* whereas a goal has a beginning, a middle, and an end. Team mission statements are broad, whereas goals are more specific.

Your team can map out a mission statement by following these steps:

Step 1: Brainstorm for ideas

Asking your team members for ideas immediately involves them in the team-building process. Begin by having them identify things they do well:

- ✔ What do they contribute to the organization that no one else can provide?
- ✔ What makes them special?
- ✔ What would the organization lose if they left?

These questions will encourage team members to think ab
they influence your organization. Once they realize that the
vital part of the organization, they will begin to visualize y
team's mission. So at this point, solicit their views on your t
mission by asking the following question:

- ✔ What is our main "*purpose*" as a team?

Remember, successful brainstorming is when people freely offer all of their thoughts on an issue; so refrain from criticizing team members' ideas. It's important for somebody to write down *all* ideas that are generated by your team. Ideas that initially seem absurd might prove invaluable after further consideration.

Step 2: Analyze the ideas

After your team has finished brainstorming, evaluate the merit of each idea that was generated. A purposeful mission statement can be created only if you allow your team members to thoroughly consider all the ideas that were presented.

Joel asked his team members . . .

to evaluate their ideas. *"We've all presented our ideas on what we think our team's mission should be. Now, we need to agree on the value of each point,"* said Joel. And so, for the next thirty minutes, the team debated the merit of each point. Afterwards, Joel concluded, *"O.K., we know now which points we agree are important. So, at our next meeting, we'll take the best ideas and combine them into a single mission statement.". . .*

Step 3: Draft a mission statement

The next step is to take your team's best ideas and draft a mission statement. Since this is a draft, don't worry if it's not perfect. Just take into account your team members' ideas and your own sense of purpose for your team. Then present your sample mission statement and ask for reactions and any changes that would improve it.

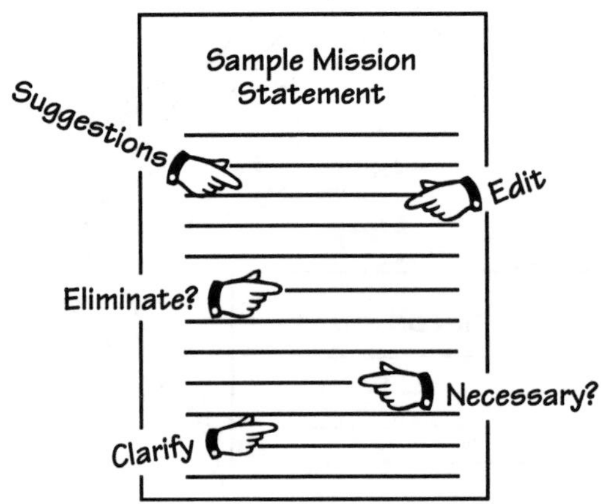

Joel thought carefully . . .

about the comments his team members offered during their first meeting. Since his department dealt primarily with customers, he decided that the sample mission statement should involve the total satisfaction of Microsales' customers.

Karen agreed immediately. The others halfheartedly nodded. *"I don't think that's the whole picture,"* John responded. *"If our mission is to satisfy customers 100 percent, we could do that by giving them some really expensive freebies when they're not happy with us. But that would defeat our purpose. When Microsales stops making a profit, we could be out of work."*

"You've brought up a good point," Joel said. *"Do you have any ideas about how we can expand our mission statement to include the organization's goals?"*. . .

Team involvement in the formulation of your mission statement is critical to identifying your team's purpose. Your mission statement needs to be approved by every team member.

Step 4: Finalize and commit to the mission statement

Reword your mission statement with your team's help. Every word may not completely satisfy all the members, but you must agree on the basic statement. Then, ask for a verbal commitment from each of your team members. To solidify their commitment, visually display the mission statement and refer to it on a regular basis.

The sales and marketing team . . .
finally agreed upon a mission statement: *"To fully satisfy every customer while we further our organization's goals."* Marlee felt that the statement was a bit too general, but she agreed with it after Joel assured her that the specifics would emerge when the team chooses their goals.

Each team member verbally agreed to the statement, and Joel made copies of the written statement. *"Please post these in your offices,"* he requested. *"It'll remind us to focus on our mission."*. . .

Once you've mapped out your team's mission statement, you're ready to chart your team's goals and priorities.

Chart Your Team's Goals And Priorities

Now that you've identified your mission, you can chart the specific goals that will help you fulfill your mission. You've chosen the mountain you need to climb; charting your goals and priorities ensures that all team members take the same path up that mountain. And if you're careful in choosing your goals, your path won't take you on unproductive detours.

As always, it's important to involve your team members in the decision-making process. Brainstorm, discuss, and assess ideas for goals that complement your mission.

The sales and marketing team . . .

had many ideas on specific goals to focus on. Armando began recording the team's comments on the flip chart. *"Not so fast,"* he advised. *"I can only write with one hand at a time."* By the end of the session, the team cut down the list to a manageable size. The following is their list. . . .

A mission is different from a goal; a mission is a clear statement of *"why your team exists,"* whereas a goal has a beginning, a middle, and an end. Team mission statements are broad, whereas goals are more specific.

Your team can map out a mission statement by following these steps:

Step 1: Brainstorm for ideas

Asking your team members for ideas immediately involves them in the team-building process. Begin by having them identify things they do well:

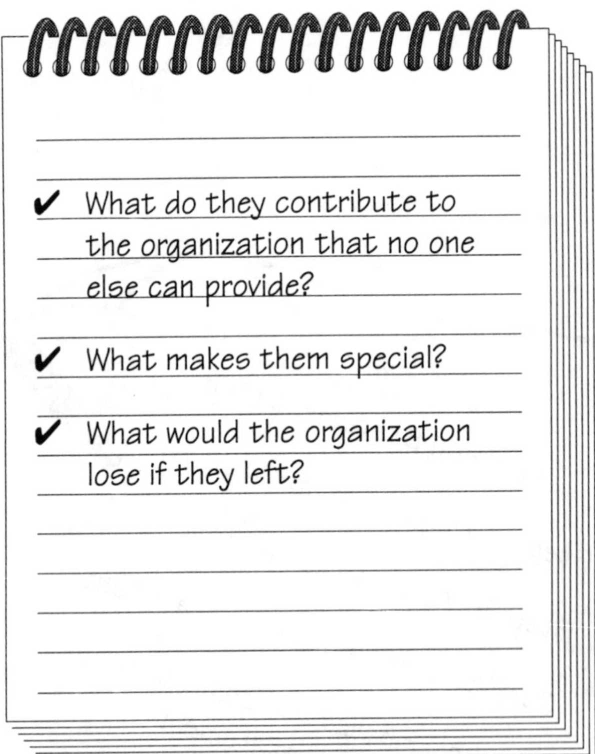

These questions will encourage team members to think about how they influence your organization. Once they realize that they're a vital part of the organization, they will begin to visualize your team's mission. So at this point, solicit their views on your team's mission by asking the following question:

✔ What is our main "*purpose*" as a team?

Remember, successful brainstorming is when people freely offer a of their thoughts on an issue; so refrain from criticizing team members' ideas. It's important for somebody to write down *all* ideas that are generated by your team. Ideas that initially seem absurd might prove invaluable after further consideration.

Joel was ready . . .

for his team's first brainstorming session. He knew his group's morale was low, so he had positive statements about each employee already prepared. Joel began the meeting with a flip chart that listed each team member's name: Marlee, John, Sue, Armando, and Karen.

"Okay, team," he said. *"Before we focus on our mission, let's focus on our part in this organization. What things can you think of that we do well?"* Silence prevailed. *"Well, I'll start us off,"* Joel said. *"Marlee and John, both of you have been with Microsales for a long time. I don't think anyone can match your explanations of our computer systems."*

"Until they dumped all the new components on top of us at once," Marlee complained. *"I can't even think straight anymore."*

Joel nodded. *"I realize that the changes have been very difficult for all of us,"* he said. *"But why don't we try to focus on just the positives right now."*

Joel looked over at Sue. *"Sue has a tremendous capacity for handling detail. She'll uncover information on anything you ask her about. And Armando, your patience is exemplary. You're able to deal with the crankiest customers without losing your cool."* Joel paused and motioned at Karen. *"As for Karen, what a fast learner! She's been here only three months, yet she already has a firm understanding of all of our products."*

The session picked up. Joel asked more pertinent questions about their team's mission, and the team members started participating. They came up with several ideas, all of which Joel recorded on the flip chart. . . .

Step 2: Analyze the ideas

After your team has finished brainstorming, evaluate the merit of each idea that was generated. A purposeful mission statement can be created only if you allow your team members to thoroughly consider all the ideas that were presented.

Joel asked his team members . . .

to evaluate their ideas. *"We've all presented our ideas on what we think our team's mission should be. Now, we need to agree on the value of each point,"* said Joel. And so, for the next thirty minutes, the team debated the merit of each point. Afterwards, Joel concluded, *"O.K., we know now which points we agree are important. So, at our next meeting, we'll take the best ideas and combine them into a single mission statement."*. . .

Step 3: Draft a mission statement

The next step is to take your team's best ideas and draft a mission statement. Since this is a draft, don't worry if it's not perfect. Just take into account your team members' ideas and your own sense of purpose for your team. Then present your sample mission statement and ask for reactions and any changes that would improve it.

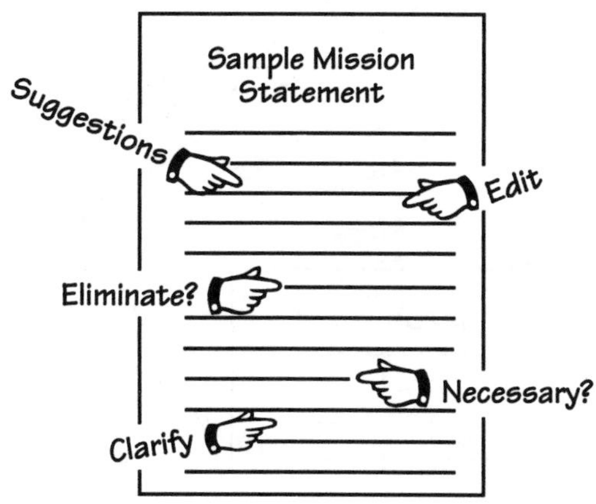

Joel thought carefully . . .

about the comments his team members offered during their first meeting. Since his department dealt primarily with customers, he decided that the sample mission statement should involve the total satisfaction of Microsales' customers.

Karen agreed immediately. The others halfheartedly nodded. *"I don't think that's the whole picture,"* John responded. *"If our mission is to satisfy customers 100 percent, we could do that by giving them some really expensive freebies when they're not happy with us. But that would defeat our purpose. When Microsales stops making a profit, we could be out of work."*

"You've brought up a good point," Joel said. *"Do you have any ideas about how we can expand our mission statement to include the organization's goals?"*. . .

Team involvement in the formulation of your mission statement is critical to identifying your team's purpose. Your mission statement needs to be approved by every team member.

Step 4: Finalize and commit to the mission statement

Reword your mission statement with your team's help. Every word may not completely satisfy all the members, but you must agree on the basic statement. Then, ask for a verbal commitment from each of your team members. To solidify their commitment, visually display the mission statement and refer to it on a regular basis.

The sales and marketing team . . .

finally agreed upon a mission statement: *"To fully satisfy every customer while we further our organization's goals."* Marlee felt that the statement was a bit too general, but she agreed with it after Joel assured her that the specifics would emerge when the team chooses their goals.

Each team member verbally agreed to the statement, and Joel made copies of the written statement. *"Please post these in your offices,"* he requested. *"It'll remind us to focus on our mission."*. . .

Once you've mapped out your team's mission statement, you're ready to chart your team's goals and priorities.

Chart Your Team's Goals And Priorities

Now that you've identified your mission, you can chart the specific goals that will help you fulfill your mission. You've chosen the mountain you need to climb; charting your goals and priorities ensures that all team members take the same path up that mountain. And if you're careful in choosing your goals, your path won't take you on unproductive detours.

As always, it's important to involve your team members in the decision-making process. Brainstorm, discuss, and assess ideas for goals that complement your mission.

The sales and marketing team . . .

had many ideas on specific goals to focus on. Armando began recording the team's comments on the flip chart. *"Not so fast,"* he advised. *"I can only write with one hand at a time."* By the end of the session, the team cut down the list to a manageable size. The following is their list. . . .

Once you've agreed on your goals, your job is to prioritize and clarify them. Consider the following:

- Which goals should you accomplish first?
- What is involved in reaching those goals?
- When can you reach them?

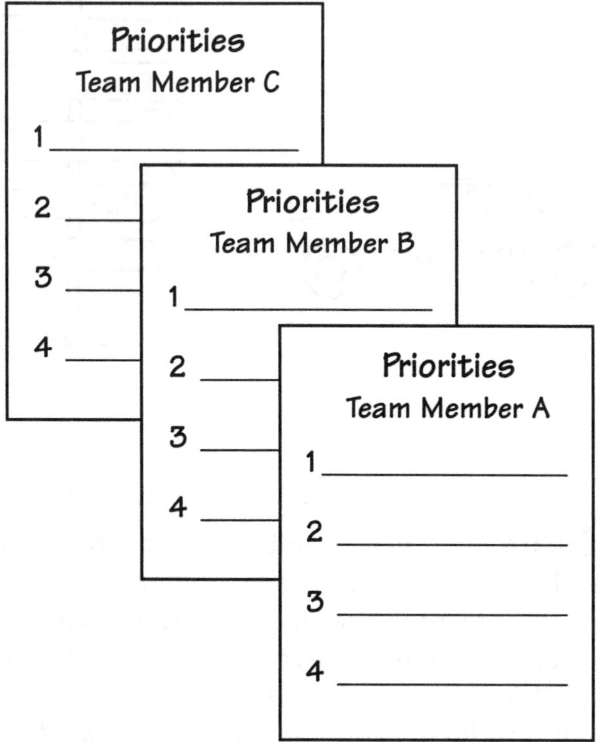

The team members decided . . .

that learning about the new products, revising the order-entry form, and assisting each other were the most important goals for their department. Designing new marketing literature fit into their mission, but the other three goals were more essential to their own capabilities. Revising the order-entry form would be the easiest to accomplish, so the group decided to fulfill that goal within the month. . . .

Once you've mapped out your team mission statement and charted your goals, you need to register your *"rules of the road."*

Register Your "Rules Of The Road" (Guidelines)

If you desire to build a dynamic team, your team has to establish certain guidelines. These guidelines are your rules of the road—rules that will maintain a productive team environment and dictate how you work together as a team.

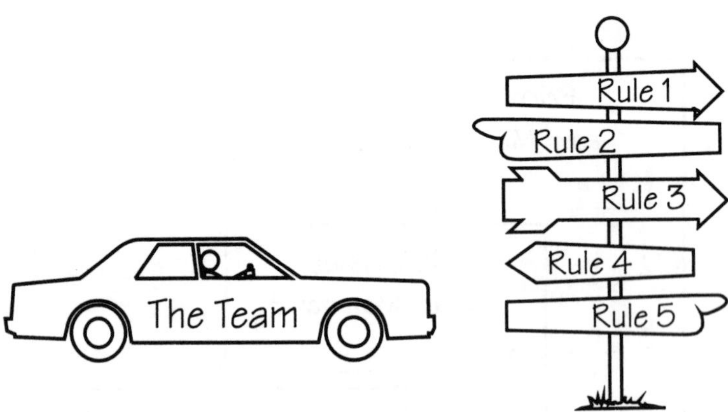

Many teams err by eliminating this step. They rush into assigning tasks and work for their team members before they've even decided how they are going to work together. Setting down guidelines for your team is like starting out on a car trip with well-defined rules: each traveler is clear regarding expectations *(e.g., each person will drive in two-hour segments, there will be a break after each person completes his or her driving segment, no loud talking allowed, etc.).* Give your team an advantage by registering its rules of the road.

The sales and marketing team members . . .

decided on the following rules of the road:

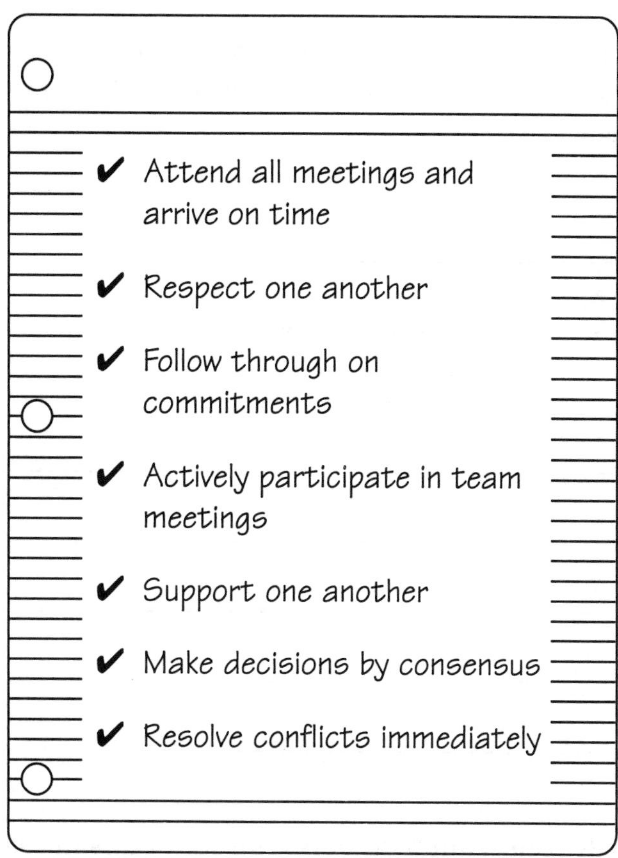

Joel typed up the list . . .

and each team member signed it. The team members agreed to leave the list open-ended, in case they determined later on that other rules were necessary.

Driving toward a mission, the first phase of building a dynamic team, is essential to every team's success. Mapping out your team's mission statement, charting your team's goals and priorities, and registering your rules of the road will sharply define your team. You'll gain commitment and forge a profitable team relationship. Fasten those seat belts—you're ready for Phase Two!

Chapter Five Worksheet: Driving Your Team's Direction

1. Draft a sample mission statement for your team. Then, with your team's help, agree on a final version of the mission statement.

2. How will your team members commit to this mission?

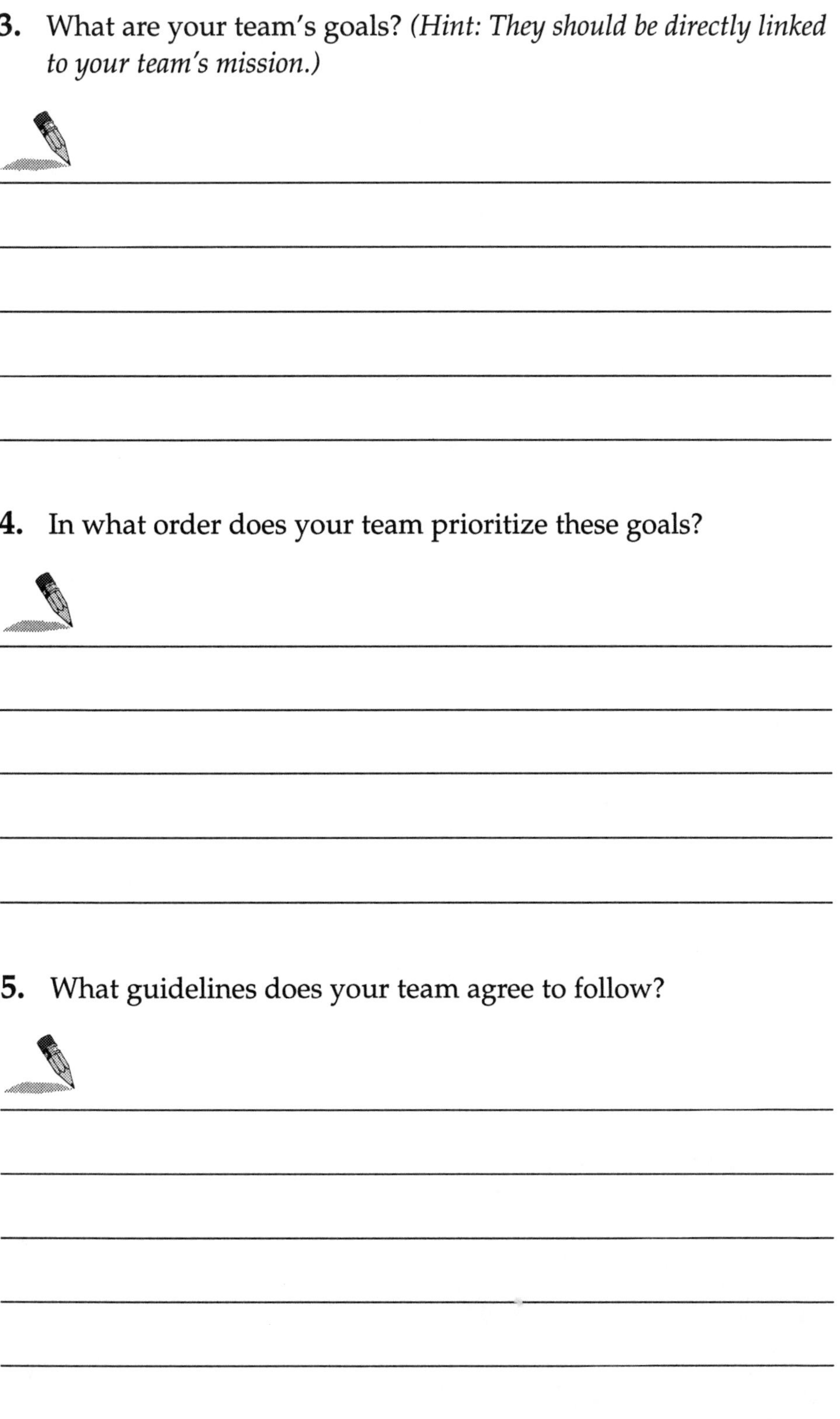

3. What are your team's goals? *(Hint: They should be directly linked to your team's mission.)*

4. In what order does your team prioritize these goals?

5. What guidelines does your team agree to follow?

Phase Two: Striving For Team Effectiveness

After Phase One, your team is at the base of the mountain, map in hand. You know where you're going, and what stops you have to make along the way. In Phase Two, you need to:

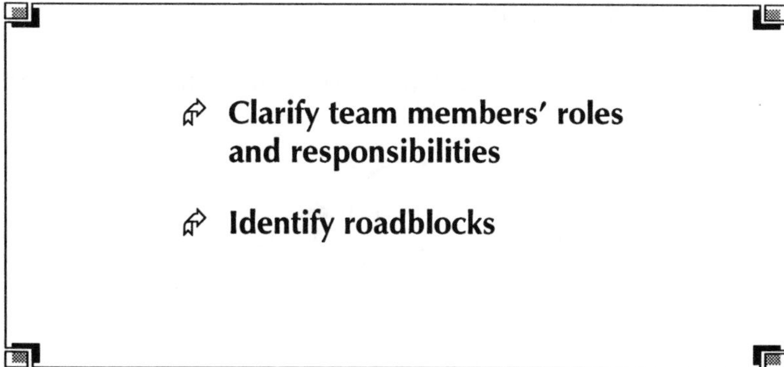

- **Clarify team members' roles and responsibilities**
- **Identify roadblocks**

Clarify Team Members' Roles And Responsibilities

A dynamic team can tackle goals much more effectively than any one individual. To hike up this segment of the mountain, you have to identify roles and responsibilities:

- Who is responsible for leading the team?
- Do you need to identify a team member responsible for communicating with other departments?
- Which tasks will each member be responsible for?

By clarifying individual roles and responsibilities, your team will know what it takes to reach success. Team members won't be *"left in the dark,"* each stumbling his or her own way up the mountain.

The two types of roles that require clarification are those that involve a specific task and those that involve the team process *(how the team members function in meetings, for example).*

Clarifying roles that relate to a specific task helps your team reach a particular goal faster and with greater ease. You can eliminate overlapping assignments, gaps in task completion, responsibility evasion, and unmet deadlines.

Clarifying roles that relate to the team process helps your team

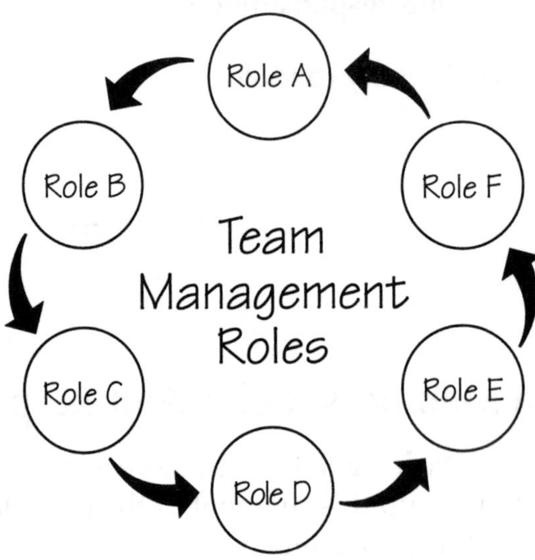

work better. For example, you can save time by not having to ask for volunteers at each meeting if one team member continually serves as the team *"recorder"* and another as the *"timekeeper."* Or you can eliminate some potential problems by having one team member function as a *"facilitator."* Depending on your team size, you can have each member function in a different role or have each member volunteer for a number of varied roles.

Joel and the rest of the . . .

sales and marketing team assigned each individual a team management role. Karen was chosen to be the team's recorder. She would be responsible for listing all ideas the team generated, as well as for recording any decisions the team made. Sue volunteered to keep time and alert the team members when they needed to speed up their discussions. John offered to act as an opinion-generator; he would focus on soliciting comments about certain issues.

To keep the team's emotions from escalating, Armando signed up as the team's facilitator. When a conflict arose, he would warn the team. This would prompt the team to resolve their conflict before it undermined the team's goals. Marlee took on the role of evaluator. She would evaluate each meeting and report any agenda items that weren't covered sufficiently. Joel was to lead the team, prepare an agenda for each meeting, and communicate the team's progress to upper management. . . .

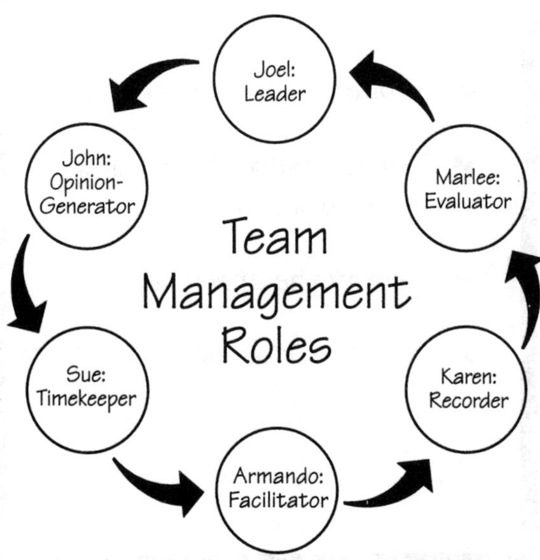

You may decide that your team needs members to take on different roles than the ones you've selected. Part of clarifying roles and responsibilities involves determining which roles are necessary. You may discover later on that your team members need new or different roles.

Whether you are attempting to clarify the responsibilities in managing your team or those that enable your team to reach a particular goal, consider the following guidelines:

Involve all team members

Remember, your team may not want an authoritarian leader. A team only functions as a real team when all members participate, not when they're told what to do. You can't expect dynamic results if you decide their responsibilities for them. If you let the team members collectively decide on their responsibilities, their commitments to the team will increase.

Joel came into the next meeting . . .

with a list of the team's goals. *"Remember our goals?"* he asked the team members.

"How could we forget?" Marlee quipped. *"You talk about them all the time. I'm surprised you haven't taped them to our telephones."* The team laughed.

"I like that idea," Joel responded. *"Maybe I'll implement it after this session. But for now, we're going to decide how each of us can help in reaching our first goal, revising the order-entry form. We set an end-of-the-month deadline for that goal. So we need to get right on it."*. . .

Express expectations and anticipations

Not everyone sees a task or responsibility in exactly the same way. You need to express the expectations and anticipations of each task before it is assigned. Then you should examine exactly what needs to be done to accomplish each task. Your team needs to ask:

- ✔ What do we expect to accomplish?
- ✔ What concerns need to be addressed to accomplish our goal?

"Let's pick apart our goal," . . .

Joel began, *"and see how we should proceed."* He held up a copy of the current order-entry form. *"What's wrong with this form? Why do we need to revise it?"*

John spoke first, *"Because the new components are listed in alphabetical order by brand name. If a customer wants a price on a fax/modem, we have to look through the whole form to find the different fax/modems we carry. It takes time, and I can't guarantee that I'll quote every fax/modem we have available."*

"So the list needs to be categorized?" Joel asked. John nodded.

Sue entered the discussion by bringing up a different point, *"The components should also be listed in order of price. Sometimes a customer wants me to quote the least expensive item we carry."*

"Maybe we need a quote sheet in addition to the order-entry form," Marlee suggested. *"We never needed one before because we only carried the basic systems, but I think it's time we came up with one."* The team members continued discussing their expectations. . . .

Identify the specifics

After your team has identified its expectations, it's time to define the specifics: what tasks need to be done and who will be responsible for each. Then you'll know what it takes to reach your goal and who will help your team succeed.

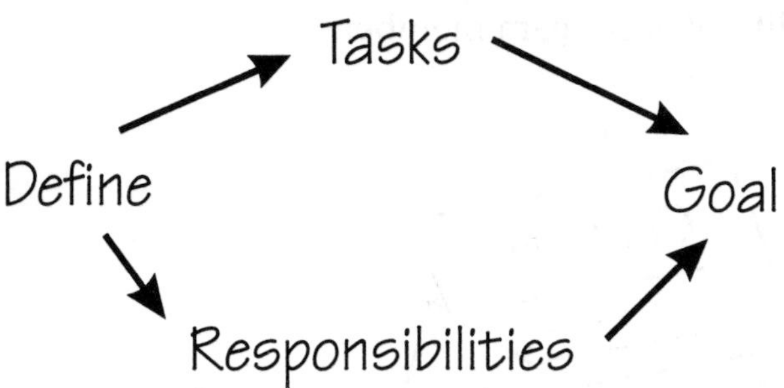

The sales and marketing team . . .
discovered that their original goal of revising the order-entry form had expanded to include an additional task: developing a quote sheet for easy reference. The quote sheet would list the categorized components in order of price. The order-entry form would list the components alphabetically within their specific categories.

The team members came up with their list of tasks and negotiated their roles. Sue and John would complete the quote sheet; Armando and Marlee were responsible for revising the order-entry form. By the end of the month, each group would give their completed assignments to Karen, who agreed to proofread and print the final versions within one week. Joel had three days to share the results with upper management; then he'd report upper management's reactions to the team members at their next scheduled meeting. . . .

Address accountability

Once you've settled on specific roles and responsibilities, you and your team members will be able to see how each individual affects the overall success of your team. Your team's prosperity depends on every member fulfilling their role. Just as every member committed to the team mission statement, each member should also commit to their own specific responsibilities. Put all commitments in writing; a signed *"contract"* will strengthen the accountability of each team member.

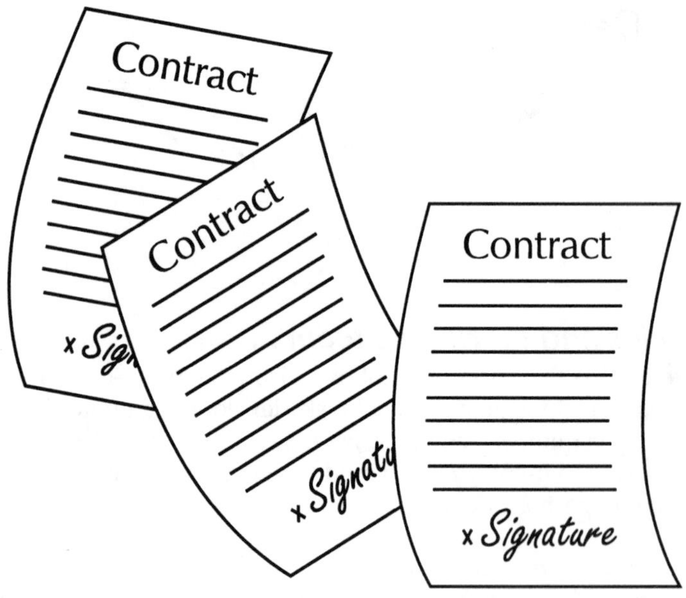

Joel asked Karen, . . .

the team's new recorder, to tear the sheet that listed the members' responsibilities off the flip chart. Joel signed first, then asked the team members to commit to their roles by also signing their names. *"I've got it on paper,"* Joel said, *"so you can't plead ignorance. If you forget what you're supposed to do, come to me. I'll show you the list."*

Identify Roadblocks

It's usually in this phase that symptoms of poor teamwork can be identified. The key is not only to note the symptoms of poor teamwork, but to cure the underlying causes. Otherwise they can destroy what you have already built: the framework of a dynamic team. You'll no doubt encounter some of the following roadblocks, but you can avoid them with proper preparation.

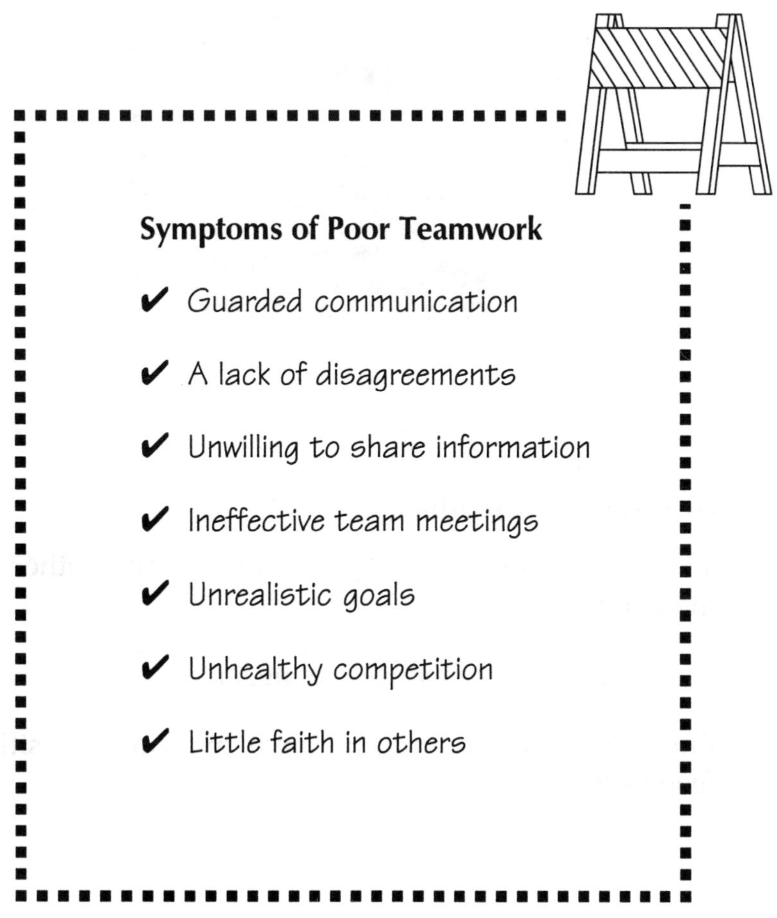

Guarded communication

If team members feel that they will be punished or receive negative reactions from freely sharing their ideas, they'll tend to say little or be extremely cautious about what they do say. They may also preface what they say with: *"perhaps," "this is only a possibility," "I heard someone say,"* etc.

How to overcome this roadblock:

- Take note of your own responses and those of other team members.
- Ask whether the responses are negative.
- Encourage open communication by providing positive feedback.

A lack of disagreements

When team members disagree, it's usually because of different perspectives on the same issue. These differences often produce ideas you never considered before. If your team members rarely disagree, it's possible that they are masking their true feelings or are unwilling to share their ideas.

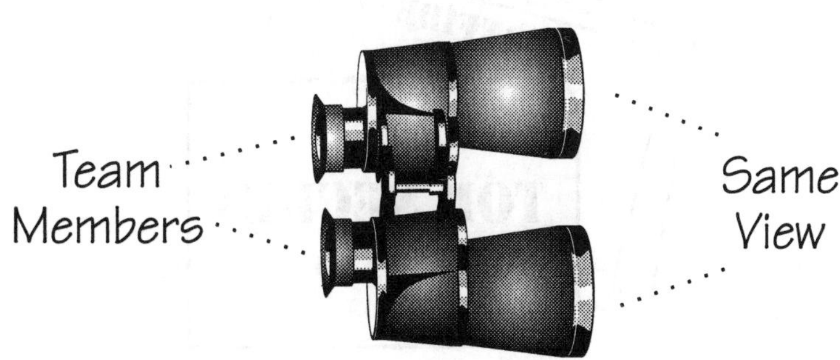

How to overcome this roadblock:

- Present disagreement as a positive experience for your team members.
- If you disagree with somebody's idea say, *"That's an important way to view this idea. My thoughts are slightly different . . ."* and then share your view.
- Don't ever attack a team member's ideas.

Unwilling to share information

Team members often have information or experience that would help in solving a problem or coming to a decision. When these team members hold back pertinent information, the team loses.

How to overcome this roadblock:

- Share information with your team. If team members don't see their leader being open with them, they might not disclose relevant information or their own ideas.
- Make sure your team members know you value their expertise or experience.
- When team members do share, appreciate their contributions.

Ineffective team meetings

Meetings reveal how a team is progressing. If you notice any of the following symptoms in your meetings, you should make changes immediately.

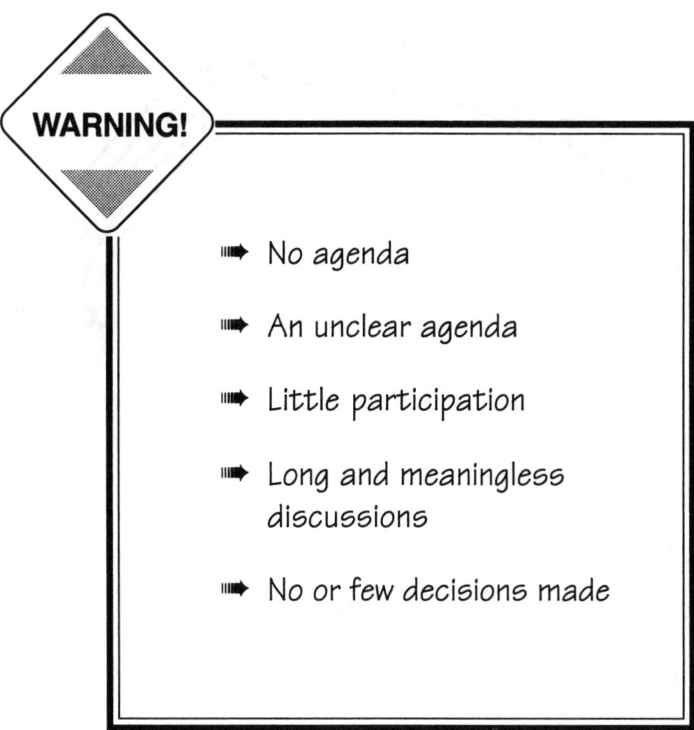

How to overcome this roadblock:

- Make sure you have a clear agenda.
- Structure your meetings and never go overtime, if at all possible.
- Don't let discussions drag on.
- Provide opportunities for all members to participate and make decisions.

Unrealistic goals

Ineffective teams set unreasonable goals; such goals require more than the team can deliver.

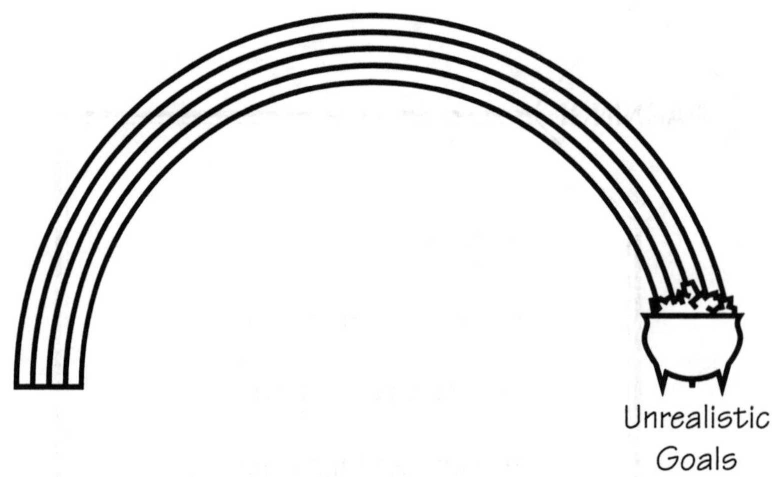

How to overcome this roadblock:

- Receive input from all of your team members.
- Identify their expectations.
- Set goals that they feel are attainable.

Unhealthy competition

Healthy competition occurs when a team strives to reach goals as a collective whole. Perhaps the team is trying to prove its worth and compete with other teams.

Unhealthy competition is the result of team members competing with each other by discrediting others, holding back information, etc. When team members who are discussing achievements pepper their speech with a lot of *"I"* statements, be on the lookout for unhealthy competition.

How to overcome this roadblock:

- Stress teamwork! Your team should be competing as a team, not as individuals against each other.
- Reliance on other team members should be built into the tasks and goals you set for your team.

Little faith in others

Individuals who are members of a dynamic team trust that all members will fulfill their roles. An ineffective team suffers from members who don't have confidence in their fellow team members. When this problem arises, productivity suffers.

How to overcome this roadblock:

- As a leader, you must set a tone of confidence.
- Continually affirm each team member's worth, and they'll soon understand that *everyone* is essential to the team's success.

Striving for team effectiveness, the second phase of building a dynamic team, provides the impetus to move your team up the mountain. Clarifying the roles and responsibilities of your team members will push them forward, and identifying common roadblocks will move your team past the pitfalls.

Don't turn back now—you're making progress!

CHAPTER SIX WORKSHEET: STRIVING FOR TEAMWORK

1. Assign each team member a role that you think they'd like to do and that they would be proficient in.

2. At your next team meeting, follow the procedure for clarifying roles and responsibilities, and see how close you came to identifying the roles for each of your team members.

3. Have any of the following roadblocks surfaced in your team development process? *(Place a check by each you've experienced.)*

For those you've checked, what might your team do to overcome them or prevent them from recurring?

❑ Guarded communication

____

____

____

____

❑ A lack of disagreements

____

____

____

____

❑ Unwilling to share information

____

____

____

____

❑ Ineffective team meetings

❑ Unrealistic goals

❑ Unhealthy competition

❑ Little faith in others

Phase Three: Thriving On Teamwork

By the end of Phase Two, your team's momentum should have increased so that your team is now quickly scaling the mountain. At first, this may be exciting, but the thrill of adventure can often vanish when the day-to-day duties become tedious and your fellow adventurers start to annoy you. You have the choice of either backsliding or making an extra effort to push your team up the mountain.

You've formed your team mission statement, chosen goals, and set down your team guidelines. You've clarified the roles and responsibilities of your team members, in both team management and individual assignments. Now, in Phase Three, you must instill the effort necessary to make your team produce.

To thrive as a team, your team will have to:

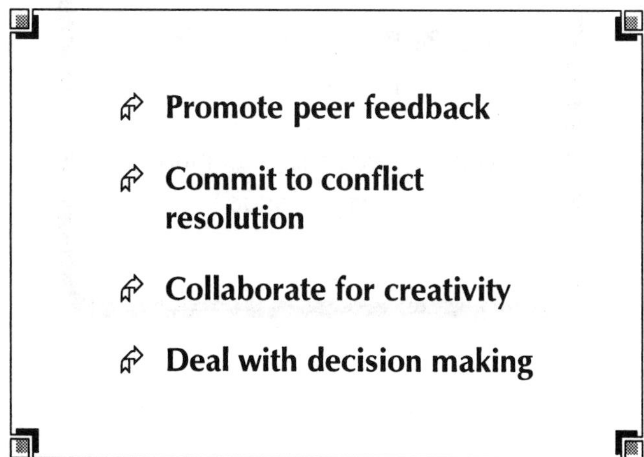

- **Promote peer feedback**
- **Commit to conflict resolution**
- **Collaborate for creativity**
- **Deal with decision making**

These might be difficult steps, but a team focused on becoming dynamic will take them.

Promote Peer Feedback

Creating an environment that encourages members to meet team goals requires peer feedback. Without feedback, either positive or negative, team members lack inspiration to improve or excel.

The following four-step process will help you promote peer feedback:

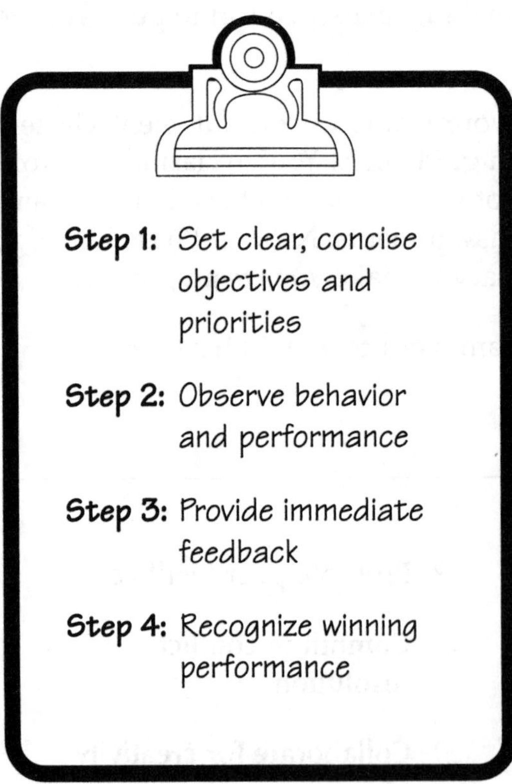

Step 1: Set clear, concise objectives and priorities

In Phase One of building a dynamic team, you discovered the necessity of setting priorities for each team member. Doing so helps team members focus on the team's goals and enables them to experience a greater degree of success. If your priorities are clear and concise, it'll be easier to give constructive feedback. Since you'll know each team member's responsibilities, your feedback can be objective and succinct.

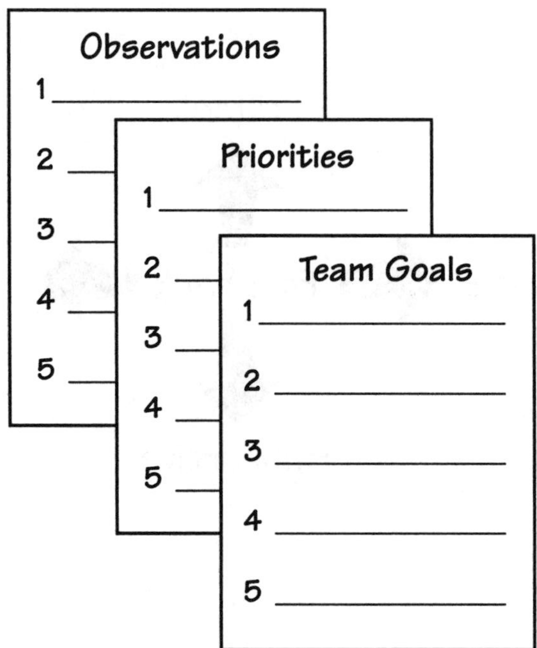

Step 2: Observe behavior and performance

You can't provide feedback unless you personally observe how your fellow team members perform. Don't ignore this step. If you provide feedback based on hearsay or your own expectations, your team members will sense your lack of substantial evidence, and you'll end up defeating your purpose.

Step 3: Provide immediate feedback

Don't wait too long to provide feedback. If you hesitate in providing feedback, your potential to direct or inspire will decrease. If your feedback is primarily positive and you wait to deliver it, the team member to whom you're providing feedback will question your interest and/or sincerity. If your feedback contains constructive criticism and you put it off, the team member might wonder why you even bothered.

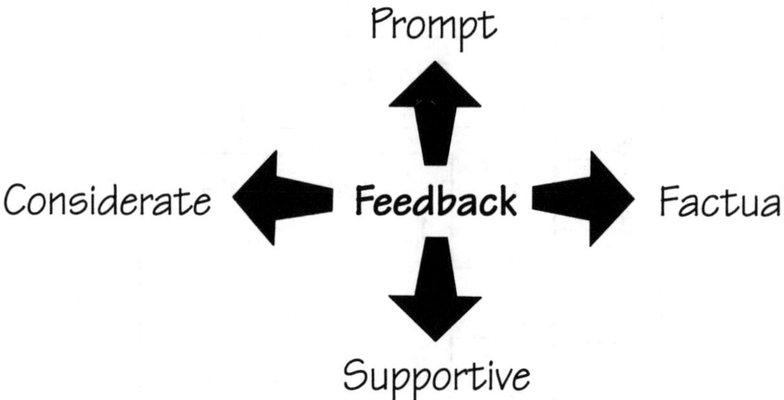

Your immediate feedback should also be factual, supportive, and considerate.

Step 4: Recognize winning performance

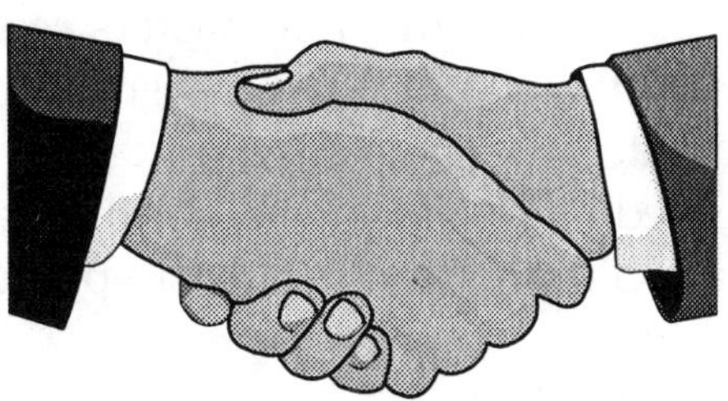

Recognizing the successful completion of objectives will help ensure that your fellow team members continue performing well. Possible ways of recognizing each others' winning performance include going out to lunch or praising a certain team member for an accomplishment.

If you are encouraging team members to provide feedback on other team members, make sure everyone is comfortable with verbally recognizing other team members' contributions.

Joel kept a close watch . . .

on his team members, asking them how they were proceeding with the quote sheet and the order-entry form. Sue and John began work on the quote sheet immediately. Joel took periodic looks at their progress and was pleased to see that they went beyond their task of categorizing the components and listing them in order of price. They also researched each component and added a short, pertinent description for the sales and marketing team.

Joel called them into his office. *"Sue, John,"* he began, *"I've noticed your diligent work on the quote sheet. Just yesterday I saw that you cut your lunch short to uncover more information about each component. That's dedication! I appreciate your work and the fact that you're helping the rest of us reach our goals. In fact, I was wondering if you could share the information you've learned about the components at our next team meeting."* John and Sue agreed, and Joel thanked them again for their help. . . .

Commit To Conflict Resolution

Every successful team masters conflict resolution—they manage conflict so that it doesn't disrupt the team, cause factions, or impede progress. A dynamic team learns to resolve disagreements immediately; otherwise, conflict can fester over time, changing a team climate from healthy to poor.

If you notice conflict between two members on your team, intervene quickly as a third party. In a closed meeting with the two team members, ask each to write their responses to the following questions: *(Encourage them to answer with positive statements only—no name-calling or derogatory remarks are allowed.)*

Opinion Worksheet

It is my opinion that he *(she)* should:

____

____

It is his *(her)* opinion that I should:

____

____

It is my opinion that I should:

____

____

It is his *(her)* opinion that he *(she)* should:

____

____

This worksheet will help the team members realize that perceptions of individuals often differ, and that opinions aren't necessarily based on fact. After the two team members have finished filling out their worksheets, work with them on transforming their responses into objectives that are agreeable to both. Then decide how they can achieve their objectives. Who will do what and when?

At the next team meeting . . .

Joel relayed the progress John and Sue had made on the quote sheet. They distributed copies that Karen had proofed, and spent twenty minutes going over additions that other team members made. The team members agreed that the quote sheet would make their jobs easier. *"Great job,"* Joel said. Then he turned to Marlee and Armando, *"How are you coming on the order-entry form?"*

Marlee pointed at Armando. *"Maybe you should ask him. He's not holding up his part of the bargain."* Armando shrugged. *"I don't think that's true,"* he responded. Joel immediately stopped this exchange. *"Why don't we talk about it after the meeting,"* he suggested.

After the meeting, Joel handed Marlee and Armando an opinion sheet. *"Apparently there's a conflict of opinion here. I'd like you to answer these questions and then we'll talk about your answers. There's only one stipulation: no negative remarks."*

The opinion sheets revealed Marlee and Armando differed on their division of tasks. Armando thought they were going to revise the form together. Marlee was under the impression that Armando would categorize the items and she'd alphabetize them and type them up. *"Actually, it's my fault,"* Joel said, *"because we didn't clarify your specific tasks at our meeting."* Together they divided the task into separate duties and set a new deadline. . . .

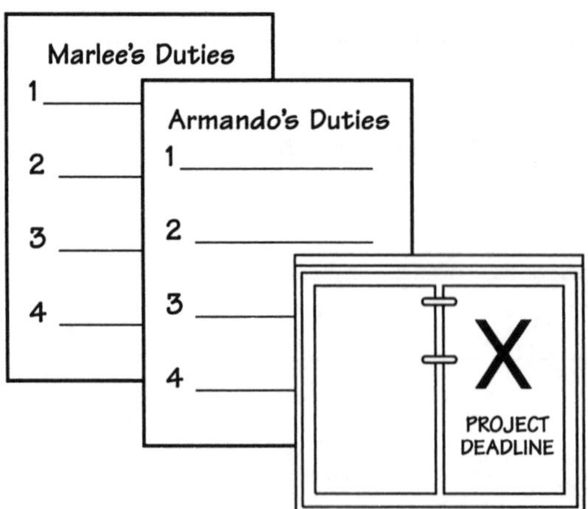

Note: *Success Through Teamwork,* a guidebook that deals specifically with team dynamics, details six guidelines to help your team manage conflict. Those guidelines will take you step-by-step through conflict resolution. If conflict resolution is a skill your team definitely needs to master, *Success Through Teamwork* is a valuable supplement to use.

Collaborate For Creativity

Successful teamwork always involves collaboration. Teams that utilize all members to their fullest capacities understand collaboration. When all team members work together during team meetings, creative ideas abound and innovations occur.

You can encourage collaboration if you create an environment where there are no restrictions on ideas. Different, unusual ideas are given free reign; no one disapproves. In such an open atmosphere, work is an exciting adventure.

Here are some tips to create an environment that rewards collaboration:

- Respond with interest to what your team members say
- Don't berate unconventional ideas
- Record all ideas
- Encourage team members to cultivate their ideas
- Request a large number of ideas
- Respect silence
- Alter perceptions
- Break your routine

Respond with interest to what your team members say

If team members know that others are interested in their ideas, it will encourage them to speak up and offer their suggestions.

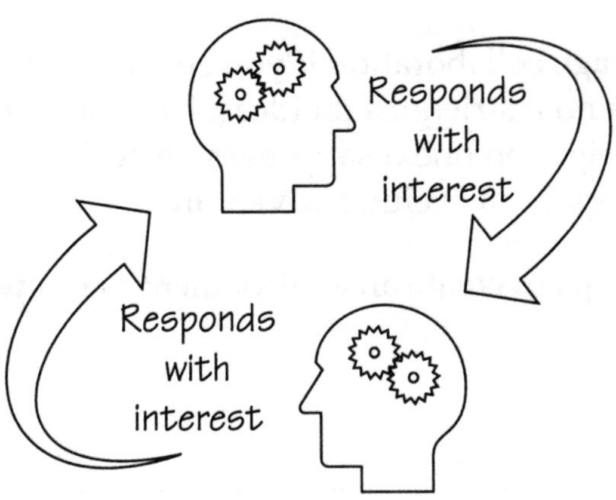

Don't berate unconventional ideas

Often, an unusual idea proves extremely useful. Learn to delete the following phrases from your team vocabulary: *"Are you kidding? Come on!" "They'll never buy that." "We'll never make it work." "Let's be more logical."*

Record all ideas

Sometimes an interesting idea gets lost because no one wrote it down. Make sure that your team recorder lists all ideas, not just the ones your team thinks are important.

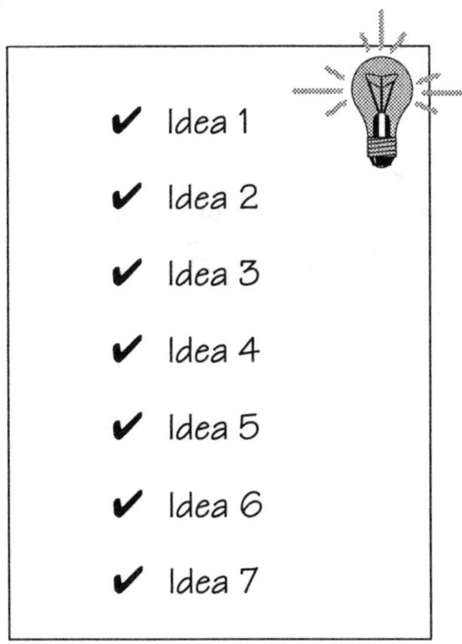

Encourage team members to cultivate their ideas

No idea is fully developed when it is first considered. Ask team members to take their *"half-baked"* ideas and envision what they could become.

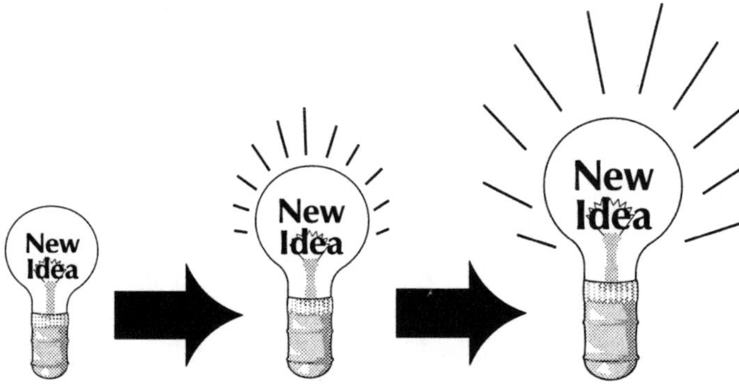

Request a large number of ideas

The bigger the pool of ideas you have to draw from, the more likely you'll come up with a winner.

Respect silence

Silence doesn't mean your team members are sleeping. Often they are thinking about an idea. Also, if it seems that you're stretching for new ideas, sometimes a break will help. Or you might want to continue that particular discussion at your next team meeting.

Alter perceptions

Get your team members out of a rut by addressing a problem in a completely different way. Have them draw the problem or act it out. Or try asking *"What if . . . ?"* questions.

Break your routine

A difference in routine will often open the floodgates of creativity. Sit on the floor, convene outside, drink lemonade, or give everyone a bell and have them make music.

At their next team meeting . . .

Joel handed out bottles of bubbles and asked the team members to take five minutes to *"release tension."* It took the team by surprise; for a few seconds the bottles stayed on the table. Then Karen cracked off the lid of her bottle and started puffing. The rest of the team soon joined in.

Joel called *"time"* after five minutes. *"Now I'm going to split us into two groups. Marlee, Karen, and Armando, you're one team; John, Sue, and I will be the other. Nobody is allowed to talk. I'm going to blindfold Marlee and Sue. They are going to try to blow bubbles, but they can't see or use their hands. Each team's goal is to help either Marlee or Sue blow the most bubbles in three minutes."*

This exercise really excited the team members. After three minutes, neither team could identify a winner, since everyone was concentrating on helping either Sue or Marlee and were too busy laughing. *"This may seem like a silly way to start our meeting,"* Joel said, *"but I wanted to prove a point and help us brainstorm. Our next team goal is to discover how we can assist each other in our respective jobs. We all have areas of weakness, where we're blindfolded and need assistance. And we all have areas of strength, where we can provide help to a blindfolded colleague. We need to figure out how we can best help each other."*

The team's break in routine proved a success. The exercise got the team thinking, and Karen could hardly record all of the ideas they generated. . . .

Deal With Decision Making

Being able to make decisions is empowering. You're able to mold the future. In every team, decisions have to be made, and those who make the decisions have control over the team.

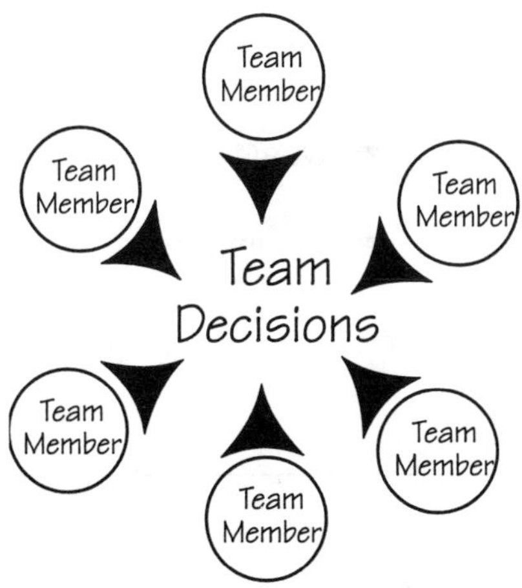

Who makes the decisions?

If the leader makes all the decisions for his/her team, the power shifts away from the people. This is a traditional decision-making hierarchy. The team members reluctantly go along with whatever the leader decides, which in turn affects how the decision is carried out. Team members feel less committed to the decision and less responsible for its outcome.

In some teams, the leader makes all the decisions after he or she consults with everyone on the team. Because of the additional input, the decision may be better, and commitment may increase to some extent, but optimum productivity is rarely achieved.

Many teams realize the effectiveness of an inclusive decision-making style, where all team members participate in the decision. In this situation, the team members come to a consensus on the decision and are therefore more committed to it. They feel responsible for carrying it out.

The characteristics of a good decision

A good decision has two characteristics:

- Quality
- Commitment

Quality

A quality decision is a logical one, backed by sound reasoning. If you've made a quality decision, you've considered the following questions:

- Have all sides of the issue been addressed?
- Have all team members been consulted?
- Do we need to contact others from outside the team for more information or advice?

Commitment

A decision that involves commitment is one that has the backing of every team member. If your decision is endorsed by your team members, you've considered the following questions:

- Do all team members agree with the decision?
- Do my team members understand their part in carrying out this decision?
- Will my team members enthusiastically carry out the decision?

The sales and marketing team . . .

reached a consensus regarding their goal of assisting each other. The team members wanted to make it easier to do their jobs well and serve their customers effectively. Input from all the team members helped them arrive at a quality decision.

They decided they would need to inventory the strengths and weaknesses of each team member. For each area, members were then paired-off; a member who was strong in an area was paired with someone who was weak in that area. For example, if Sue was having trouble with irate customers, she might be paired with Armando. He could help her with the difficult customers and teach her his techniques, thereby improving her skills. The pairs would be switched at intervals, so that each member could both train and receive training. The decision would benefit everyone, and all members were committed to carrying it out.

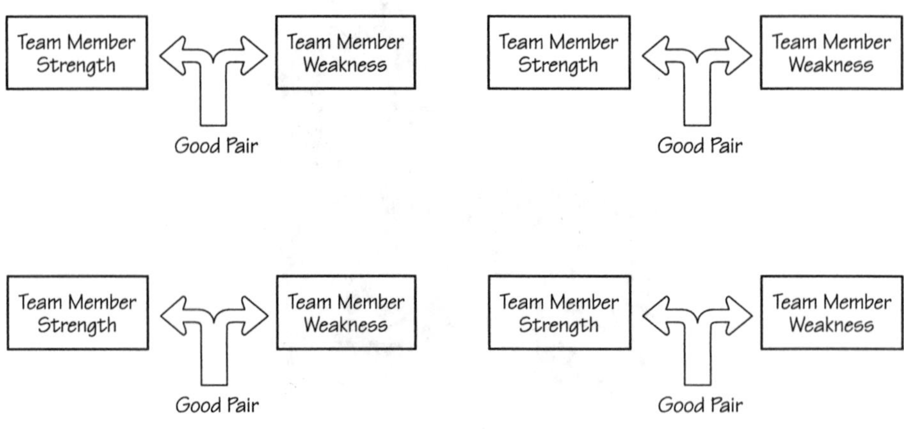

Thriving on teamwork, the third phase of building a dynamic team, has moved your team even closer to peak performance. Members are committed to resolving conflicts constructively, feedback skills have been honed, and an effective decision-making process is in place and supported. The peak is in sight!

CHAPTER SEVEN WORKSHEET: YOUR THRIVING TEAM

1. Identify one person in your team who could benefit from constructive feedback. Perhaps this person is in the midst of a project or recently finished one.

a) List your observations regarding this team member's performance.

____

____

____

____

____

____

b) Prepare a *"feedback summary"* that lists what you will say in an objective manner.

____

____

____

____

____

____

c) Decide how you will recognize the team member's performance if it is/was productive.

2. Consider the following scenario:

One of your fellow team members, Barbara, enters your cubicle and immediately starts complaining about Carl, another member of your team. *"I just can't take it anymore,"* she says. *"Carl can't do anything right. I just asked him for a report, and he handed me the wrong one! And then he had the nerve to tell me to get lost! I'm at my wit's end."*

How will you handle this conflict between Barbara and Carl?

3. List three things you can immediately do to improve the collaboration climate in your team meetings.

4. Think of a recent decision your team has made. Who made the decision? Did all team members support the decision? Did they, or are they, carry(*ing*) it out?

PHASE FOUR: ARRIVING AT PEAK PERFORMANCE

You've done it—you've reached the mountaintop. You've managed to mold an unlikely group of individuals into a dynamic, high-performance team. Your goal at this point is to maintain your hold, to keep your team members committed. If you can keep your team members in top shape, they'll be less likely to slip backwards.

Have You Really Reached the Top?

Maybe you've achieved a couple of your team's goals, resolved a number of conflicts, come up with some innovations, and established an effective feedback system. But have you really reached team *"nirvana"*? Are you running exclusively on the fuel of peak performance?

To determine whether your team is performing in Phase Four or is instead plodding through Phase Two or Three, read through the following list. If you can unconditionally agree with every statement, you've arrived at the peak.

	Agree	Disagree
1. The goals and priorities we've chosen are clear and relate well to our team's mission.	❑	❑
2. Our team members' roles and responsibilities are clear. Everyone knows who is responsible for what, and when we are expected to complete our tasks.	❑	❑
3. All team members take part in decisions, which are reached by consensus only.	❑	❑
4. We encourage participation in team discussions and we thoroughly examine each idea.	❑	❑
5. Our team members have open lines of communication.	❑	❑
6. We view mistakes as learning opportunities.	❑	❑
7. Our team develops and rewards collaboration.	❑	❑
8. If interpersonal issues arise, we confront, not overlook, them.	❑	❑

	Agree	Disagree
9. We consider conflicts normal and resolve them openly and immediately.	❑	❑
10. We have an informal approach toward problem solving; the leader is challenged as often as any other team member.	❑	❑
11. Planning is a critical element in our team process, and all members participate in it.	❑	❑
12. Our team considers diverse viewpoints.	❑	❑
13. When we say we will do something, we're committed to it.	❑	❑
14. Our team's trust level is high; we provide feedback consistently and frequently.	❑	❑

If you've stalled in responding wholeheartedly to one or more of the statements, take a closer look. Each statement hones in on one characteristic of a dynamic team. Maybe your team can receive top honors for planning and following through on a commitment, but not all of your team members participate in discussions.

Or perhaps your team members get along great and are creative participants, but it's difficult for you to accomplish anything. It might be worthwhile to review the elements of a dynamic team. It may be that your team could use a refresher course in clarifying roles and responsibilities, or they could benefit from some collaboration exercises. In any case, every team needs reviving at some point or another.

Joel's team had come a long way . . .

since its beginning. He was very pleased with the results. The team members had revised their order-entry form and formulated a quote sheet, and they had spent a considerable amount of time taking inventory of the strengths and weaknesses of each team member. Additionally, they had begun implementing their paired-assistance program and were in the midst of a training program that would increase their knowledge of the new components.

The team's efforts showed in their results: customers were more satisfied; sales had increased; the team members had less stress; and everyone worked well together. In fact, other departments noticed the enthusiasm in the Sales and Marketing department.

Then the unexpected happened . . .

Sue left the organization and Marilyn, an employee from another department, joined the team. John volunteered to take over Sue's role as timekeeper and the team members had to acclimate Marilyn to their team concept, mission, goals, and guidelines. In addition, they had to train Marilyn and inventory her strengths and weaknesses before assigning her a partner.

The loss of one member changed the composition of the team, but the members were able to *"revive"* themselves, ascend the mountain a second time, and regain their productivity. . . .

Maintaining Motivation

If you're already at peak production, it's your job to keep your team motivated. You need them to continue at their level of performance, but it's not easy to maintain such a level. We all have *"off"* days. Sometimes it only takes a downturn in the attitude of one of your team members to send your team tumbling off the mountain.

To maintain your team's productivity, consider the following *"maintenance motivators"*—tips designed to keep your team focused upward.

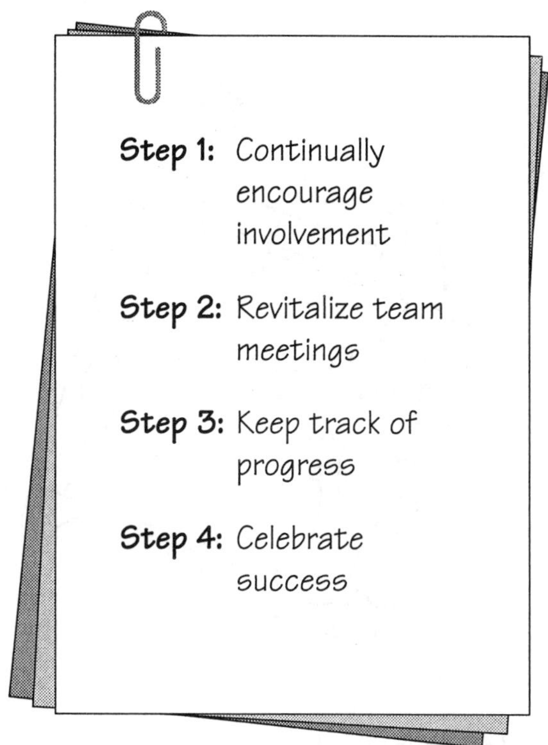

Step 1: Continually encourage involvement

After a team has been working together for a while, interest often wanes and involvement slackens. You need to reiterate to your fellow team members that their involvement is what fuels the team. Maybe the excitement of building a team has paled, but you can still motivate your team members to take part. Only motivated team members can consistently deliver exceptional results.

Think about rotating the team leadership, switching some of the routine responsibilities, allowing team members to train others, and/or providing opportunities for team members to share their expertise. In addition, keep encouraging and rewarding involvement in team discussions. Sometimes a change in your team allows you to increase involvement.

When Sue left Microsales, Inc. . . .

and Marilyn came on board, the adjustment of roles and responsibilities recharged the team. Although the change caused a delay in achieving some of their goals, it made them review and renew their commitment to the team. . . .

Step 2: Revitalize team meetings

Are your team members feeling a little bit stifled? Are your meetings boring and commonplace? Then maybe you need to revitalize your team's meetings. Review some of the collaboration tips in Chapter Seven to help revitalize your meetings. If they are too predictable, creativity will suffer. Prod your team members out of their seats and into productivity.

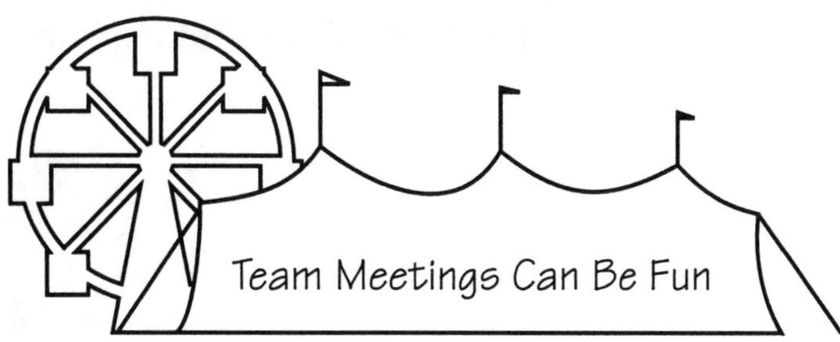

Joel realized that boring meetings . . .

wouldn't serve his purpose. So he tried some different approaches. He scheduled one breakfast meeting and asked each team member to bring his or her favorite cereal. He supplied milk, juice, bowls, and spoons. Then the team members swapped cereals and munched as they discussed designing new marketing literature. At another meeting, Joel blindfolded the team members during a discussion to help them realize how important nonvisual communication is. The team members found that innovative meetings increased their creativity. . . .

Step 3: Keep track of progress

No matter how stimulating your team meetings are, if your team doesn't make progress you'll flunk the team-performance test. And if your team is making progress, but they're not aware or reminded of it, it's harder to achieve a higher grade. Score keeping is crucial. Data doesn't lie, cheat, or make excuses. If your team is making it, you'll know.

Once you've begun making progress, bring up your team's results at each meeting. If possible, track your team's progress on a graph or chart. A visual display of progress is a great way to reinforce the fact that your team is effective. And seeing a measured response to their progress keeps team members from slipping into complacency.

Joel brought charts . . . of the team's progress to every meeting. For each goal the team established, he charted the team's progress in attaining that goal. As an additional incentive to keep the team focused on its mission, he often called up a customer during team meetings and asked for feedback. After a couple of such calls, he rotated the duty among the team members to let them personally experience feedback from the people they dealt with on a daily basis. It wasn't always positive, but it was a good learning experience for the team. . . .

Step 4: Celebrate success

Maintain your team's high performance; reward them for their achievements. Even a step in the right direction is cause for celebration. Maybe your organization can't afford bonuses or major perks, but what about swinging for a pizza party or letting team members have an afternoon off after they've reached a major goal?

Spread your success stories by telling the rest of the organization about your team's achievements. Other departments might be inspired to take action, and your team members will appreciate the publicity. They'll want to maintain their status of peak performance, because others will be watching.

One of the reasons Marilyn . . .

applied for the position in the Sales and Marketing department after Sue left was that she had heard about the team's achievements. Joel had spread the good news about his department throughout the organization, and Marilyn decided she wanted to be a part of a dynamic team.

The team members were pleased with their reputation. And when Joel was able to tabulate the increase in customer satisfaction, he managed to get a day off for each team member. They had to stagger their days to cover everybody's hours, but the members felt they had accomplished an important task and appreciated the response to their success.

Maintaining a dynamic team takes almost as much work as building one. But it can be done, and the payoffs make up for all the effort!

CHAPTER EIGHT WORKSHEET: KEEPING YOUR TEAM DYNAMIC

1. Take a few minutes to think about your team.

a) Then write a paragraph describing your team.

____

____

____

____

____

____

____

____

b) Next, look carefully at your description. Does it characterize a Phase Four team? Circle the statements that describe a Phase Four team.

____

____

c) Ask the other members to do the same. Compare notes. *(You can copy and distribute the "Keeping Your Team Dynamic" worksheet in the Appendix for their use.)*

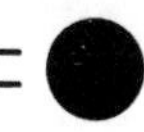

2. For each of the four maintenance motivators, list ideas you have implemented or could implement to help maintain your team's status as a dynamic team.

a) Continually encourage involvement.

b) Revitalize team meetings.

c) Keep track of progress.

d) Celebrate success.

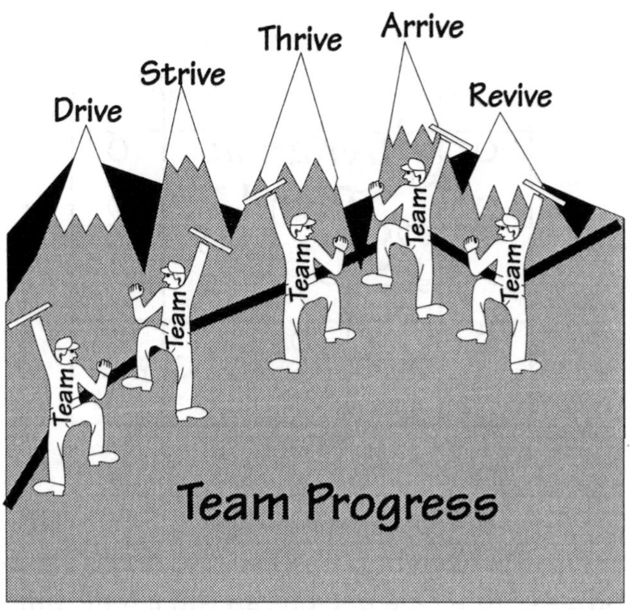

CHAPTER NINE

Building a dynamic team takes time. It requires patience, persistence, and an overwhelming desire to achieve. But you do it, step-by-step, until you reach the top. And when change throws you off a cliff, you and your team members will pick yourselves up, brush off, and attempt the climb with renewed fervor.

Why? Why take on all that work? Why not just hop on a plane and request the pilot to drop you off at the nearest peak? Because there will never be an airplane that can take you to that height. You need human effort, human reasoning, and human stamina to mold a group of individuals into a dynamic team.

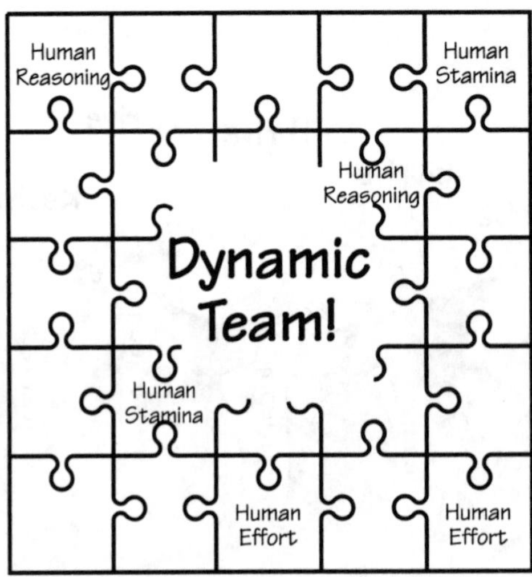

You're committed to team building because teams can conquer what individuals can't. One person can run a mile; but a relay team can run that mile faster. It's the combined effort of a committed team that reaches greater heights than any individual can dream of. It's that promise of peak performance that pushes leaders to build dynamic teams.

So give it your all!

- ☑ Drive your team toward a mission. This is the phase where your team takes on a sense of identity through the mission it establishes for itself.

- ☑ Strive with your team to clarify roles and responsibilities that take you closer to your mission. Anticipate and prepare in advance for the inevitable roadblocks. You may even be able to plot a course around them in advance.

- ☑ Thrive with your team, working diligently to experience the exhilaration of real teamwork. Teams are made up of people, people who need to know how to master conflict, provide feedback, and make decisions.

- ☑ Arrive at the peak, as a dynamic team that produces results. And don't forget to revive your team when it needs rejuvenation, that extra push to get it back on the mountain trail.

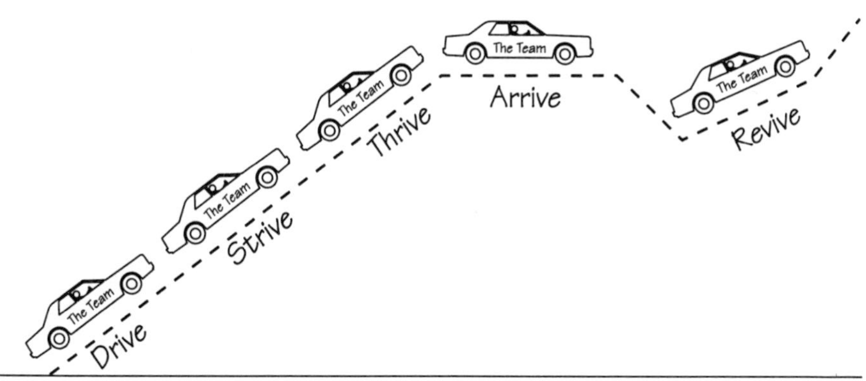

Are you ready to begin? It's an uphill climb, but it's the only one that leads to the top!

"DYNAMIC TEAM" ASSESSMENT

Use the following assessment to rate your team (*if you haven't yet formed a team, rate a team you were previously on*). For each characteristic of a dynamic team, rate your team on a scale of 1 to 7; circling a "7" means your team is exceptional, and a "1" means it is deficient.

"Dynamic Team" Assessment

1. Clearly states its mission and goals

1 2 3 4 5 6 7

2. Operates creatively

1 2 3 4 5 6 7

3. Focuses on results

1 2 3 4 5 6 7

4. Clarifies roles and responsibilities

1 2 3 4 5 6 7

5. Is well-organized

1 2 3 4 5 6 7

6. Builds upon individual strengths

1 2 3 4 5 6 7

7. Supports leadership and each other

1 2 3 4 5 6 7

8. Develops team climate

1 2 3 4 5 6 7

9. Resolves disagreements

1 2 3 4 5 6 7

10. Communicates openly

1 2 3 4 5 6 7

11. Makes objective decisions

1 2 3 4 5 6 7

12. Evaluates its own effectiveness

1 2 3 4 5 6 7

Total Score ________________

Interpreting your score:

If your score is 75–84: Congratulations! Your team is at, or near, optimum performance. Maintaining your team at this high level should be your goal.

If your score is 65–74: Not bad! Your team's in pretty good shape, although there is room for improvement.

If your score is 55–64: Your team has problems, some of which may be serious. To rectify them, your team needs to focus on improving its lowest-scoring characteristics.

If your score is 54 or below: Your members are not functioning as a team. Your team needs to work on the basics of team building.

Opinion Worksheet

It is my opinion that he *(she)* should:

It is his *(her)* opinion that I should:

It is my opinion that I should:

It is his *(her)* opinion that he *(she)* should:

KEEPING YOUR TEAM DYNAMIC

1. Take a few minutes to think about your team.

a) Then write a paragraph describing your team.

b) Next, look carefully at your description. Does it characterize a Phase Four team? Circle the statements that describe a Phase Four team.

c) Ask the other members to do the same. Compare notes.

2. For each of the four maintenance motivators, list ideas you have implemented or could implement to help maintain your team's status as a dynamic team.

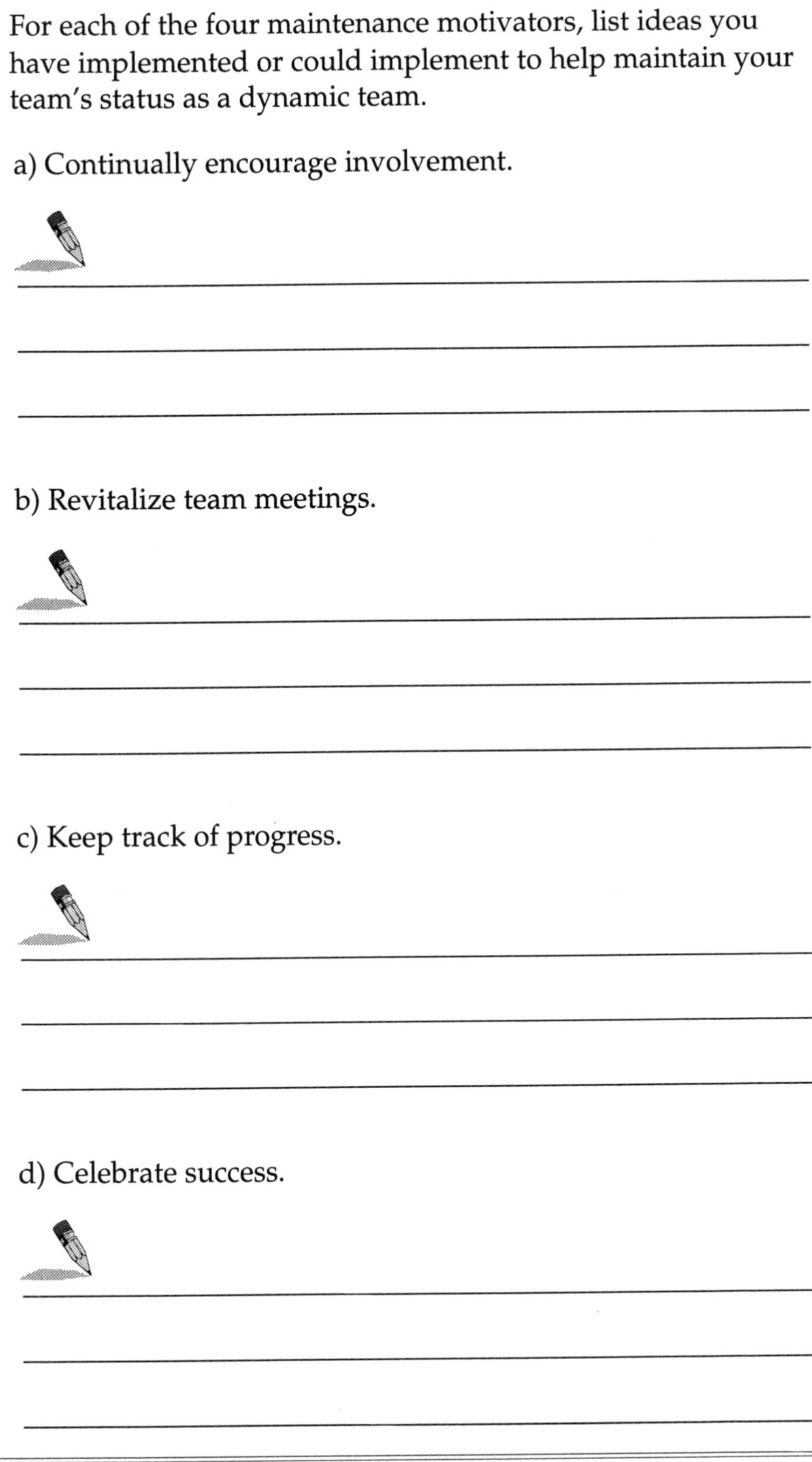

a) Continually encourage involvement.

b) Revitalize team meetings.

c) Keep track of progress.

d) Celebrate success.

THE PRACTICAL GUIDEBOOK COLLECTION

QUALITY IMPROVEMENT SERIES

- Meetings That Work!
- Continuous Improvement Tools Volume 1
- Continuous Improvement Tools Volume 2
- Step-By-Step Problem Solving
- Satisfying Internal Customers First!
- Continuous Process Improvement
- Improving Through Benchmarking
- Succeeding As A Self-Managed Team
- Reengineering In Action

MANAGEMENT SKILLS SERIES

- Coaching Through Effective Feedback
- Expanding Leadership Impact
- Mastering Change Management
- Effective Induction And Training
- Re-Creating Teams During Transitions

HIGH PERFORMANCE TEAM SERIES

- Success Through Teamwork
- Team Decision-Making Techniques
- Measuring Team Performance
- Building A Dynamic Team

HIGH-IMPACT TRAINING SERIES

- Creating High-Impact Training
- Identifying Targeted Training Needs
- Mapping A Winning Training Approach
- Producing High-Impact Learning Tools
- Applying Successful Training Techniques
- Measuring The Impact Of Training
- Make Your Training Results Last

Evaluation and Feedback Form

We need your help to continuously improve the quality of the resources provided through the Richard Chang Associates, Inc., Publications Division. We would greatly appreciate your input and suggestions regarding this particular guidebook, as well as future guidebook interests.

Please photocopy this form before completing it, since other readers may use this guidebook. Thank you in advance for your feedback.

Guidebook Title: ____________________

1. Overall, how would you rate your *level of satisfaction* with this guidebook? Please circle your response.

Extremely Dissatisfied		Satisfied		Extremely Satisfied
1	2	3	4	5

2. What specific *concepts or methods* did you find *most* helpful?

____

____

3. What specific *concepts or methods* did you find *least* helpful?

____

____

4. As an individual who may purchase additional guidebooks in the future, what *characteristics/features/benefits* are most important to you in making a decision to purchase a guidebook *(or another similar book)*?

____

____

5. What additional *subject matter/topic areas* would you like to see addressed in future guidebooks?

____

____

Name *(optional)*:

Address: ____________________

C/S/Z: ____________________ **Phone (   )** ____________________

Please Fax Your Responses To: (714) 756-0853 USA
Or (0171) 837-6348 UK

EVALUATION AND FEEDBACK FORM

We need your help to continually improve the quality of [illegible] Richard C[illegible] Associates plc. Publications [illegible] your input and suggestions regarding this [illegible]

[illegible]